STUDY GUIDE WITH PRACTICE TESTS

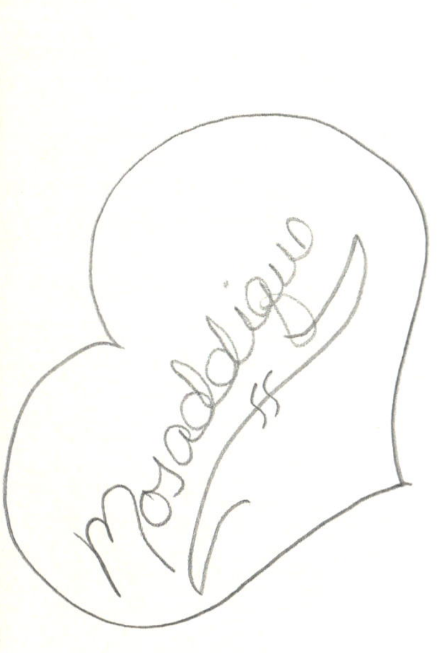

STUDY GUIDE WITH PRACTICE TESTS

STEPHEN R. SCHMIDT
CONSTANCE R. SCHMIDT

Virginia Polytechnic Institute & State University

PSYCHOLOGY:

Principles and Applications

Stephen Worchel

Wayne Shebilske

PRENTICE-HALL, INC., Englewood Cliffs, New Jersey 07632

ISBN 0-13-732354-9

Printed in the United States of America

10 9 8 7 6 5 4 3 3 1

Prentice-Hall International, Inc., *London*
Prentice-Hall of Australia Pty. Limited, *Sydney*
Editora Prentice-Hall do Brasil, LTDA, *Rio de Janeiro*
Prentice-Hall Canada Inc., *Toronto*
Prentice-Hall of India Private Limited, *New Delhi*
Prentice-Hall of Japan, Inc., *Tokyo*
Prentice-Hall of Southeast Asia Pte. Ltd., *Singapore*
Whitehall Books Limited, *Wellington, New Zealand*

CONTENTS

PREFACE

This *Study Guide with Practice Tests* is designed to accompany *Psychology: Principles and Applications*, by Worchel and Shebilske. Obviously, there is no substitute for a careful reading of textbook material. However, the guide should aid you in mastering the material in the text in three general ways. First, the guide will help you organize the material in the text by highlighting the key concepts. Second, the guide will provide you with several opportunities for testing your grasp of those key concepts. Finally, the guide will challenge you to go beyond the information presented in the text and apply it to real-world problems and situations.

Each chapter in the guide corresponds to a chapter in the text. The chapters are divided into five sections:

1. *Chapter Outline:* A detailed outline of the main points and concepts presented in the chapter.

2. *Chapter Objectives:* A list of goals you might adopt prior to reading the chapter. The goals will be listed in the form: "You should be able to . . . after completing this chapter."

3. *Key Terms Self-Test:* An opportunity to test your grasp of the definitions of key chapter terms.

4. *Practice Tests:* A series of multiple-choice questions followed by a list of the correct answers.

5. *Thought Questions/Applications:* Questions and problems that challenge you to go beyond factual information, make inferences, you relate your newly acquired knowledge to everyday problems and situations.

vii

STUDY GUIDE
WITH PRACTICE TESTS

1

Introduction

CHAPTER OUTLINE

CHAPTER OBJECTIVES

After completing Chapter 1, you should:

1. Be able to give a general description of the field of psychology.

2. Know the roots of structuralism, and be able to describe the method of analytic introspection.

3. Be able to distinguish between the structuralist school and functionalism.

4. Know the basic premise of the Gestalt school of psychology.

5. Know why the behaviorist approach to psychology focuses on observable events.

6. Understand the basic differences between the psychoanalytic and the humanistic schools of psychology.

7. Be able to explain how psychology is made up of major fields and subfields of study and understand the interrelations among these subfields.

8. Have some idea of the variety of employment opportunities available to psychologists.

9. Know what a case history is, and know some of the weaknesses of this method of investigation.

10. Describe what kind of variables one can control by using a survey method.

11. Know what kind of information can be derived from psychological tests.

12. Know the strengths and weaknesses of naturalistic observation.

13. Understand why causation cannot be inferred from correlation.

14. Distinguish between a laboratory experiment and a field experiment.

15. Know under what conditions one can make statements concerning cause and effect relationships.

16. Be able to recognize several strengths and weaknesses of the experimental method.

17. Know that psychological investigation often raises ethical issues, and that these issues must be dealt with in some form before an investigation is carried out.

KEY TERMS SELF-TEST

In each group below, fill in the letter of the term on the right with the appropriate definition on the left.

Schools of Psychology

Definitions

Key Terms

E _____ 1. the scientific study of behavior

A _____ 2. emphasized the function of thought

B _____ 3. German school based on the premise that we experience wholes

F _____ 4. based on identifying the elements of human experience

D _____ 5. emphasized the role of unconscious thoughts, fears, and wishes

C _____ 6. based on the premise that human behavior can be described in terms of observable stimuli and responses

a. functionalism (p. 6)
b. Gestalt (p. 6)
c. behaviorism (p. 6)
d. psychoanalytic (p. 8)
e. psychology (p. 1)
f. structuralism (p. 5)

Subfields of Psychology

Definitions

 1. examines the function of age on behavior

 2. examines the behavior and cognition that are related to learning, memory, perception, motivation, and emotion

 3. focuses on individual differences

4. the study of the way in which people are affected by social situations and relationships

 5. studies the neurobiological events that underlie learning, memory, and so forth

 6. dedicated to the diagnosis and treatment of emotional and behavioral disorders

Key Terms

a. experimental psychology (p. 10)
b. physiological psychology (p. 10)
c. personality psychology (p. 14)
d. clinical psychology (p. 14)
e. developmental psychology (p. 13)
f. social psychology (p. 13)

Research Methods

Definitions

 1. uses questionnaires that are given to large samples of people

2. an idea that is tested experimentally

3. looks in depth at a few individuals or a single event

 4. designed to identify individual differences among people

 5. variable manipulated in an experiment

 6. expectation on the part of the person running an experiment which can effect the outcome of the experiment

7. involves studying reactions to naturally occurring events in natural settings

Key Terms

a. experimenter bias (p. 25)
b. independent variable (p. 23)
c. hypotheses (p. 18)
d. psychological test (p. 21)
e. case history (p. 20)
f. theory (p. 18)
g. naturalistic observation (p. 22)
h. dependent variable (p. 23)
i. survey (p. 20)
j. experiment (p. 23)

_____ 8. explanation about why a behavior
          occurs

_____ 9. the variable that is measured in an
          experiment

_____ 10. an investigation in which a researcher
           directly manipulates one variable
           while measuring the effects on some
           other variable

Answers to Key Terms Self-Test

Schools of Psychology

1. e   4. f
2. a   5. d
3. b   6. c

Subfields of Psychology

1. e   4. f
2. a   5. b
3. e   6. d

Research Methods

1. i   6. a
2. c   7. g
3. e   8. f
4. d   9. h
5. b   10. j

PRACTICE TEST

Circle the correct letter.

1. The field of psychology is aimed at (p. 4):
   a. discovering people's inner thoughts and feelings.
   b. explaining the behavior of rats and pigeons.
   c. discovering the "hows and whys" of behavior.
   d. discovering the origin of human experience.

2. Which of the persons listed below started the first psychological laboratory and was the founder of structuralism (p. 4)?
   a. B. F. Skinner
   b. E. B. Titchner
   c. W. Wundt
   d. J. Dewey

3. Emphasis on the function of thought led the ___________________ to pursue important applications in education (p. 6):
   a. functionalists
   b. empiricists
   c. structuralists
   d. educational psychologists

4. Gestalt psychology derived its name from the German word meaning (p. 6):
   a. arrangement.
   b. whole.
   c. organization.
   d. observation.

5. Which of the following persons is not associated with the behaviorist movement (p. 7)?
   a. John Watson
   b. B. F. Skinner
   c. Kohler
   d. All the above are behaviorists.

6. Which of the following schools of psychology emphasized unconscious motivating forces as determinants of human behavior (p. 8)?
   a. behaviorist
   b. psychoanalytic
   c. humanist
   d. functionalist

7. According to the humanist school, people are (p. 9):
   a. driven by destructive forces.
   b. basically good.
   c. dominated by environmental stimuli.
   d. strongly influenced by their early relationship with their parents.

8. The subfields of physiological and experimental psychology are concerned with (p. 10):
   a. learning and memory.
   b. perception.
   c. motivation and emotion.
   d. all of the above.

9. Which of the following subfields is concerned with studying neurobiological events underlying behavior (p. 10)?
   a. experimental psychology
   b. physiological psychology
   c. cognitive psychology
   d. developmental psychobiology

10. Experimental psychologists use animals in research because (p. 11):
   a. they are easier to handle than humans.
   b. they enable powerful manipulations and fine controls.
   c. mental events to not intervene between a stimulus and an animal's response.
   d. the white rat is the "mascot of the field."

11. If you were interested in discovering the "programs" which govern behavior (like the programs of an Atari game), you would be a(n) (p. 12):
    a. experimental psychologist.
    b. physiological psychologist.
    c. cognitive psychologist.
    d. computer scientist.

12. Which of the following questions would not be of central concern to a developmental psychologist (p. 13)?
    a. when a child first smiles
    b. the influences of a divorce on a child's development
    c. changes that take place in elderly adults
    d. All of the above are of interest to a developmental psychologist.

13. Research findings from social psychology have been used to (p. 13):
    a. help select juries.
    b. plan advertising campaigns.
    c. design political campaigngs.
    d. diagnose and treat emotional disorders.
    e. a, b, and c.

14. Clinical psychologists are (pp. 14-15)
    a. medical doctors that specialize in psychological problems.
    b. not medical doctors.
    c. concerned with how behavior relates to our legal system.
    d. a and c.

15. If you were interested in being accepted to the Harvard Business School, you would do well to (p. 14):
    a. be a business major.
    b. be a psychology major.
    c. have a meeting with a clinical psychologist.
    d. see a school psychologist.

16. Which of the following persons would most likely be helpful in interpreting intelligence, achievement, and vocational tests (p. 15)?
    a. an experimental psychologist
    b. a counseling or school psychologist
    c. a psychoanalyst
    d. a cognitive psychologist

17. An important part of an industrial psychologist's job is to:
    a. make sure that a person's special talents are put to good use.
    b. analyze how behaviors are influenced by the weather.
    c. make human interactions with machines as comfortable as possible.
    d. promote mental health.

18. If you were interested in designing the best control panels for the operation of atomic power plants, you would consult a(n) (p. 16):
   a. industrial psychologist.
   b. environmental psychologist.
   c. control engineer.
   d. engineering psychologist.

19. Which of the following is *not* currently a subfield of psychology (p. 17)?
   a. environmental psychology
   b. forensic psychology
   c. psychology of minorities
   d. nefarious psychology

20. Which of the following methods could be used to study the relation between TV violence and violent behavior in television viewers (pp. 19-23)?
   a. case history
   b. survey
   c. laboratory experiment
   d. all of the above

21. Consider the statement: "Watching *Sesame Street* will increase a child's intelligence." (p. 18)
   a. This statement is a hypothesis.
   b. This statement is a theory.
   c. The statement can be verified by a positive correlation between time spent watching *Sesame Street* and IQ.
   d. The statement can be verified by a negative correlation between time spent watching *Sesame Street* and IQ.

22. Which of the following is a disadvantage of the case-history method of psychological investigation (p. 22)?
   a. Independent variables may be unrealistic.
   b. It is difficult to determine the relation between events studied by this method.
   c. The results may be true of only a select group of individuals.
   d. b and c.

23. Which of the following is *not* an advantage of the survey method of psychological investigation (pp. 20-21)?
   a. People often slant their answers in order to "look good."
   b. One can collect a great deal of information from a large number of people.
   c. One can select people from a number of different backgrounds.
   d. b and c.

24. A psychological test can be used to (p. 21):
    a. identify individual differences.
    b. measure attitudes.
    c. assess intellectual abilities.
    d. all of the above.

25. When a person wants to be a "good" subject and give the experimenter the "right" answer, that person is (p. 21):
    a. responding to demand characteristics.
    b. a member of the control group.
    c. showing experimenter bias.
    d. voicing a hypothesis.

26. Which of the following is characteristic of naturalistic observations (p. 23)?
    a. Subjects are randomly assigned to groups.
    b. The results do not tell us about cause and effect relations.
    c. A control group is usually necessary.
    d. The results can be easily verified by another investigator.

27. One can infer cause and effect relationships in an experiment when (p. 24):
    a. the independent variable is the only difference between groups.
    b. the dependent variable is the only difference between groups.
    c. the subject and experimenter are aware of the independent variable.
    d. the control group receives a placebo.

28. Which of the following is not an advantage of the experimental method (pp. 25-26)?
    a. An experiment can be repeated by anyone who may wish to verify it.
    b. Experiments can be used to analyze variables precisely.
    c. In an experiment, subjects know that they are being studied.
    d. All of the above are advantages of the experimental method.

29. As a psychological investigator, one must be concerned with (pp. 26-27):
    a. the anonymity of subjects in the investigation.
    b. what a person learns about himself during an investigation.
    c. possible harmful consequences of participation in the investigation.
    d. all of the above.

30. Compared to a laboratory experiment, a field experiment (p. 27):
    a. gives one more control over the situation.
    b. is less likely to run into ethical problems.
    c. makes the independent and dependent variables more realistic.
    d. all of the above.

1. c	16. b
2. c	17. a
3. a	18. d
4. b	19. d
5. c	20. d
6. b	21. a
7. b	22. d
8. d	23. a
9. b	24. d
10. b	25. a
11. c	26. b
12. d	27. a
13. e	28. c
14. b	29. d
15. b	30. c

THOUGHT QUESTIONS/APPLICATIONS

1. Chapter 1 began with a description of Hondo's life. In this description we learned about Hondo's personality, about differences between people, and (hopefully) something about psychological inquiry. Would you consider this description a case study? Why or why not? What psychological principles were demonstrated in this description?

2. The subfields of psychology can sometimes be traced to particular schools of psychology. For example, much of the work in experimental psychology can be traced to the behaviorists. To what schools of psychology would you trace clinical psychology, industrial psychology, and cognitive psychology? Defend your answers.

3. As you saw in Chapter 1, there are many different methods of psychological investigation. Each method has its strengths and weaknesses. Also, each method is best suited to answer particular types of questions. Which method do you think is best suited for the clinical psychologist? Which is best suited for the social psychologist?

4. A number of ethical issues are raised in Chapter 1. These issues are of concern when all types of human subjects are used. What additional, special issues might arise if an investigation involves young children, the mentally handicapped, or the emotionally disturbed?

2

Biology and Behavior

CHAPTER OUTLINE

CHAPTER OBJECTIVES

After completing Chapter 2, you should:

1. Understand how bodily functions are often the result of a complex interaction between the nervous system and the endocrine system.

2. Know the basic structure of the neuron and how the neuron functions to transmit electrical impulses.

3. Understand some of the chemical processes involved in synaptic transmission.

4. Know the basic structure of the brain in terms of the hindbrain, midbrain, and forebrain.

5. Understand that the cerebral cortex has two hemispheres, each with specialized functions.

6. Be able to describe the basic structure of the spinal cord.

7. Be able to explain the difference between an anatomical division of the nervous system and a functional division of the nervous system.

8. Understand the complementary roles of the sympathetic and parasympathetic divisions of the autonomic nervous system.

9. Know the basic structures involved in the control of skeletal muscles.

10. Be able to describe the role of the endocrine system in the regulation of energy level, food intake, and sexual behavior.

11. Know that chromosomes are made up of many genes and how these combine to determine one's genotype.

12. Know the means by which a mutation might occur as a result of errors in gene transmission, and be able to give an example of such a mutation.

13. Be able to describe how genetic traits are determined by the combination of genes.

KEY TERMS SELF-TEST

In each group below, fill in the letter of the term on the right with the appropriate definition on the left.

Neurons

Definitions

1. cell in the nervous system that sends and receives impulses

2. short fibers extending from a neuron which receive impulses

3. an electric tension that exists in a neuron between the cells inside and the outside environment

Key Terms

a. polarizations (p. 35)
b. dendrite (p. 34)
c. chemical transmitters (p. 36)
d. neuron (p. 34)
e. synapse (p. 36)
f. absolute refractory period (p. 35)

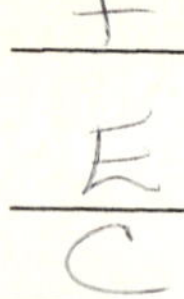 4. a period after a cell has fired, during
which it will not fire again

 5. a junction between two neurons

 6. chemicals that carry messages
between neurons

Structure of the Nervous System

Definitions

 1. part of the hindbrain; coordinates
the force, range, and rate of body
movements

 2. part of the forebrain; controls body
temperature and the rate of fat and
carbohydrate consumption

 3. part of the forebrain made up of
two hemispheres; governs advanced
human abilities

4. part of the cerebral cortex located
in front of the central fissure

5. carries sensory information up the
spinal cord

6. carries commands down the spinal
cord to move muscles

Key Terms

a. motor cortex (p. 42)
b. hypothalamous (p. 40)
c. ascending nerves (p. 44)
d. cerebellum (p. 39)
e. descending nerves (p. 44)
f. cerebral cortex (p. 41)

Functional Systems

Definitions

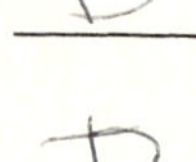 1. activates all regions of the brain;
important in controlling
alertness and attention

 2. controls emotions, memories,
and goal-directed behavior

 3. divided into sympathetic and
parasympathetic; regulates
glands and organs

Key Terms

a. Broca's aphasia (p. 50)
b. limbic system (p. 46)
c. hormones (p. 50)
d. reticular activating system (p. 46)
e. pancreas (p. 52)
f. autonomic nervous system (p. 47)
g. thyroxin (p. 51)

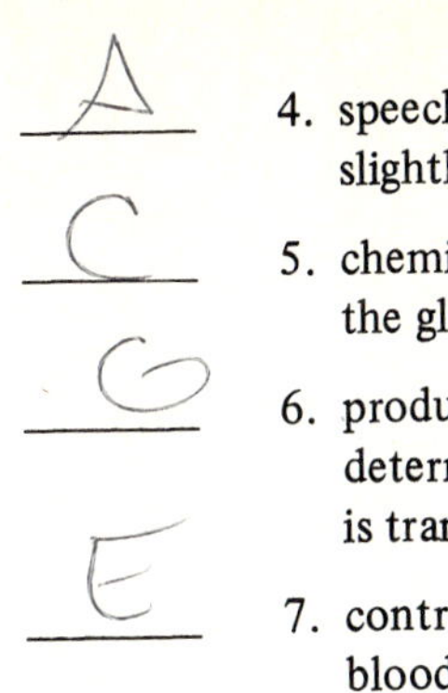

4. speech that is slow, labored, and slightly distorted

5. chemical messengers released by the glands into the bloodstream

6. produced by the thyroid glands; determines the rate at which food is transformed into energy

7. controls the level of sugar in the blood by secreting insulin and glucagon

Genetics

Definition

1. unique set of genes that we inherit from our parents

2. characterized by mental retardation and altered physical appearance

3. process in which fluid is taken from the mother's womb to test for genetic disorders

4. trait which is determined by a specific gene on its own

5. trait determined by the action of more than one gene pair

Key Term

a. polygenic trait (p. 57)
b. single-gene trait (p. 57)
c. Down's syndrome (p. 54)
d. genotype (p. 53)
e. amniocentesis (p. 54)

Answers to Key Terms Self-Test

Neurons

1. d   4. f
2. b   5. e
3. a   6. c

Structure of the Nervous System

1. d   4. a
2. b   5. c
3. f   6. e

Functional Systems		**Genetics**	
1. d	5. c	1. d	4. b
2. b	6. g	2. c	5. a
3. f	7. e	3. e	
4. a			

PRACTICE TEST

Circle the correct letter.

1. Neurons are similar to other cells in that they have (p. 34):
   a. a cell nucleus.
   b. a cell body.
   c. a cell membrane.
   d. all of the above.

2. Neurons are different from other cells in that they have (p. 34):
   a. dendrites and axons.
   b. tiny fibers extending out from their body.
   c. a cell nucleus.
   d. a and b.

3. Some axons have a fatty covering called (p. 35):
   a. a membrane.
   b. a mylin sheath.
   c. a synaptic covering.
   d. vesicles.

4. Neurons have an "on" state and an "off" state. The on state is called a state of

   _______________, while the off state is called a state of _______________ (p. 35):
   a. deplorization, polarization.
   b. polarization, depolarization.
   c. refractory period, resting period.
   d. none of the above.

5. A neuron can send different messages by (p. 36):
   a. changing the strength of its response.
   b. changing the threshold of its response.
   c. changing the rate of its response.
   d. Neurons work in an all-or-none fashion and thus can send only one type of response.

6. ________________________ ___________________________ occurs as impulses move from
   one neuron to another (p. 36):
   a. Synaptic transmission
   b. Axonal transmission
   c. Dendrite transmission
   d. Chemical transmission

7. Which of the following is not a part of the synapse (p. 36)?
   a. axon terminal
   b. myelin sheath
   c. dendrite
   d. synaptic vesicles

8. Which of the following is not characteristic of chemical transmitters (p. 36)?
   a. They carry messages between neurons.
   b. They can excite a neuron.
   c. They can inhibit a neuron.
   d. All of the above are characteristic of chemical transmitters.

9. Synapses using _______________________ usually transmit strong fast-acting, excitatory
   messages (p. 37):
   a. catecholamines
   b. amphetamines
   c. acetylcholines
   d. synaptic vesicles

10. Which of the following *does not* have its effect by blocking the reuptake of catecholamines
    (p. 37)?
    a. myasthenia gravis
    b. benzedrine
    c. cocaine
    d. dexedrine

11. The hindbrain consists of the (pp. 38-39):
    a. medulla, pons, and cerebellum.
    b. hypothalamus, thalamus, and cerebrum.
    c. reticular formation and brainstem.
    d. frontal lobe, occipital lobe, temporal lobe.

12. The forebrain consists of the (pp. 40-41):
    a. medulla, pons, and cerebellum.
    b. hypothalamus, thalamus, and cerebrum.
    c. reticular formation and the brainstem.
    d. frontal lobe, occipital lobe, temporal lobe.

13. The cerebral cortex is divided into right and left hemispheres which are connected by the (p. 41):
    a. frontal lobe.
    b. lateral fissure.
    c. brainstem.
    d. corpus collosum.

14. The occipital lobe receives ____________________, while the temporal lobe receives

    ____________________ (pp. 41-42):
    a. sensory impulses from other lobes/touch and pain impulses.
    b. touch and pain impulses/sensory impulses from other lobes.
    c. impulses from the eyes/sound and smell impulses.
    d. sound and smell impulses/impulses from the eyes.

15. The ____________________ is directly behind the central fissure and controls sensory responses of the body (p. 42):
    a. somatosensory cortex
    b. motor cortex
    c. frontal lobe
    d. parietal lobe

16. Research with split-brain patients found that the two hemispheres of cerebrum have separate functions. The split-brain condition was the result of (p. 43):
    a. surgically cutting the corpus callosum.
    b. epileptic seizures.
    c. tumors on the occipital lobe.
    d. all of the above.

17. When split-brain patients were blindfolded, they (p. 43):
    a. could not name an object held in their left hand.
    b. could not name an object held in their right hand.
    c. could not recognize abstract words.
    d. a and b above.

18. The nerve tissue in the brain and spinal cord is called the (p. 44):
    a. central nervous system.
    b. peripheral nervous system.
    c. limbic system.
    d. autonomic nervous system.

19. Which of the following reflexes is responsible for withdrawal of the hand from a hot stove (pp. 44-45)?
    a. stretch reflex
    b. flexor reflex
    c. flexor-cross-extensor reflex
    d. startle reflex

20. Polio is a viral disease resulting in paralysis of the leg and other muscles. This disease attacks (p. 44):
    a. the brain stem.
    b. the reticular activating system.
    c. the ascending nerves of the spinal cord.
    d. the descending nerves of the spinal cord.

21. Disruption of normal functioning of the limbic system may cause (p. 46):
    a. emotional upheavals.
    b. public urination.
    c. memory lapses.
    d. all of the above.

22. The sympathetic division of the autonomic nervous system is responsible for (p. 47):
    a. the fight-or-flight responses.
    b. relaxation responses.
    c. selective attention.
    d. regulation of energy expenditure.

23. The parasympathetic division of the autonomic nervous system is responsible for (p. 47):
    a. the fight-or-flight responses.
    b. relaxation responses.
    c. selective attention.
    d. regulation of energy expenditure.

24. Which of the following is *not* a part of the motor system (pp. 49-49)?
    a. basal ganglia
    b. medulla
    c. cerebellum
    d. pyramidal cells

25. In general, the basal ganglia (p. 49):
    a. perform large, general muscle movements.
    b. control fine-grain muscle movements.
    c. set the stage for detailed, controlled movements.
    d. a and c above.

26. Wernicke's aphasia is characterized by (p. 50):
    a. speech that is slow, labored, and slightly distorted.
    b. speech that sounds normal until one pays attention to meaning.
    c. arrested mental development.
    d. difficulty understanding language.

27. The endocrine system regulates body chemistry by the release of (p. 50):
   a. hormones.
   b. ribonucleic acid.
   c. chemical transmitters.
   d. a and c above.

28. The thyroid gland produces thyroxin, a substance that (p. 51):
   a. controls the level of sugar in the blood.
   b. if too abundant, will make one burn food too fast.
   c. if too abundant, will make one sterile.
   d. if not abundant enough, will intensify one's reaction to stress.

29. The rate at which you transform food into energy is (p. 51):
   a. called the metabolic rate.
   b. called the rate of carbohydrate uptake.
   c. controlled by the pancreas.
   d. controlled by the parathyroid gland.

30. The level of sugar in the blood is controlled by the (p. 52):
   a. pancreas.
   b. pituitary gland.
   c. thyroid gland.
   d. gonads.

31. Genes are transmitted from generation to generation by means of (p. 53):
   a. gametes.
   b. zygotes.
   c. deoxyribonucleic acid.
   d. ribonucleic acid.

32. Which of the following chromosomal mutations may lead to abnormal aggressiveness (p. 54)?
   a. mutations of the 23 chromosomes of the XXY variety
   b. mutations of the 23 chromosomes of the XYY variety
   c. Down's syndrome
   d. mutations of the 21 chromosomes

33. Which of the following is probably not a cause of genetic mutations (p. 55)?
   a. the wearing of tight trousers by men
   b. mutator genes
   c. radiation
   d. All of the above have been linked to mutations.

34. A male may be colorblind if his mother is colorblind, but a female cannot inherit colorblindness from her mother alone. This is because (p. 57):
   a. colorblindness is a sex-linked trait.
   b. the colorblindness allele (c) is recessive.
   c. colorblindness is a polygenic trait.
   d. a and b above.

35. The "test-tube" baby represents an application of (p. 56):
   a. cloning.
   b. genetic engineering.
   c. gene synthesis.
   d. a and b above.

Answers to the Practice Test

1. a	13. d	25. d
2. d	14. c	26. b
3. b	15. a	27. a
4. a	16. a	28. b
5. c	17. a	29. a
6. a	18. a	30. a
7. b	19. b	31. a
8. d	20. d	32. b
9. c	21. d	33. d
10. a	22. a	34. d
11. a	23. b	35. b
12. b	24. b	

THOUGHT QUESTIONS/APPLICATIONS

1. Suppose one were to compare the functions of the human nervous system to the electrical system of an automobile. What part of the electrical system would correspond to the spinal cord, the motor cortex, and the reticular activating system? Do you see any other correspondences?

2. One of the major differences between humans and other animals is the human ability to use language. Based on this difference between species, what differences in brain structure or function would you expect between species?

3. Suppose an acquaintance of yours was in an accident and sustained a head injury. If the injury were concentrated on the left side of the head, in front of the ear, what type of deficits might you expect?

4. In the chapter it is stated that some female Russian athletes have XXY chromosome structures. Why would such a structure lead to superior athletic performance?

3

Sensation and Perception

CHAPTER OUTLINE

CHAPTER OBJECTIVES

After completing Chapter 3, you should:

1. Have a general idea of how stimuli are translated into psychological experiences that are seen, heard, tasted, smelled, or felt.

2. Be aware of the tremendous perceptual demands placed upon us in daily life and upon others in highly specialized activities such as the Apollo 13 mission.

3. Be able to contrast the functions of rods and cones in the retina.

4. Understand why we have difficulty seeing following rapid changes in illumination (for example, when we go into a dark theater from bright sunlight).

5. Be able to explain why color vision cannot be explained by simply saying there are different receptors for different colors.

6. Realize that we do not simply take our sensory input "as is"; instead, we impose organization on sensory input.

7. Understand why it is essential that the size, shape, and brightness of objects remain constant even when optical information about those objects changes.

8. Be able to list the many cues available to us for perceiving depth and understand why we are sometimes "fooled" by misleading information.

9. Know that our sensory and perceptual systems are not perfect, that sometimes illusions can occur—illusions that can have catastrophic consequences.

10. Be able to explain why the eye is *not* a camera.

11. Understand why the future for blind individuals may be "brighter" than it once was.

12. Understand how the various structures of the ear translate sound waves into neural impulses.

13. Be able to characterize sound in terms of frequency, amplitude, and waveform.

14. Be able to explain how we localize sounds in our environment.

15. Understand why perception of pain is still a mystery to scientists.

16. Realize that neither vascular theory nor specific receptor theory accounts completely for our perception of temperature.

17. Understand how we know where we are with respect to our environment and where our body parts are.

In each group below, fill in the letter of the term on the right with the appropriate definition on the left.

Vision I

Definitions   **Key Terms**

d   1. network of muscles behind aqueous humor

e   2. instrument for examining the eye's internal structure

f   3. part of the eye that helps cornea focus light onto back of eye

a   4. disease characterized by "cloudy" lenses

c   5. condition resulting when eye is flattened in shape

b   6. center area of retina where vision is best

g   7. using the sides of one's eyes to see something

a. cataracts (p. 66)
b. fovea (p. 66)
c. farsightedness (p. 66)
d. iris (p. 66)
e. ophthalmoscope (p. 66)
f. lens (p. 66)
g. peripheral vision (p. 67)

Vision II

Definitions   **Key Terms**

f   1. upward adjustment in sensitivity to light

b   2. entire range of wavelengths of electromagentic radiation

e   3. law suggesting we group elements that are close together

a   4. term describing reversal in relationship between figure and ground

a. multistable perception *or* figure-ground reversal (p. 74)
b. electromagnetic spectrum (p. 71)
c. binocular disparity (p. 78)
d. law of shape constancy (p. 77)
e. law of nearness *or* proximity (p. 74)
f. light adaptation (p. 69)
g. linear perspective (p. 78)

 5. law stating that we see an object's shape as constant when the object's slant changes

6. experience of seeing a different view from each of our eyes

7. monocular cue for depth perception used by artists to create the impression of depth

Hearing

Definitions

 1. three small bones in middle ear

2. membrane in cochlea containing hair cells

3. scientific instrument converting sound waves into visible waves

4. number of wavecrests that occur in a second

5. unit for measuring loudness

6. partial hearing loss caused by spending long periods of time around loud noises

7. sounds containing a single frequency

Key Terms

a. hammer, anvil, stirrup (p. 82)
b. pure tones (p. 85)
c. frequency of sound waves (p. 83)
d. decibel (p. 85)
e. boilermaker's deafness (p. 85)
f. oscilloscope (p. 83)
g. basilar membrane (p. 83)

Other Senses

Definitions

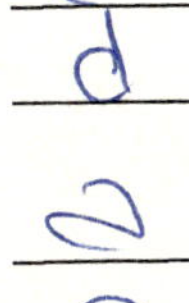 1. small elevations on the tongue

2. odor-sensitive cells in passageway between nose and throat

3. areas of the skin where only hot is felt

4. the least distance between two stimuli that can be perceived as separate on the skin

Key Terms

a. warm spots (p. 89)
b. vestibular system (p. 92)
c. semicircular canals (p. 92)
d. olfactory cells (p. 88)
e. papillae (p. 87)
f. equilibrium (p. 90)
g. two-point threshold (p. 90)

   5. our sense of overall body orientation

   6. inner-ear structure that detects body
     orientation

   7. three arching structures in the inner
     ear detecting changes in head position

Answers to Key Terms Self-Test

Vision I

1. d	5. c
2. e	6. b
3. f	7. g
4. a	

Vision II

1. f	5. d
2. b	6. c
3. e	7. g
4. a	

Hearing

1. a	5. d
2. g	6. e
3. f	7. b
4. c	

Other Senses

1. e	5. f
2. d	6. c
3. a	7. b
4. g	

PRACTICE TEST

Circle the correct letter.

1. Which of the following is *not* a major psychophysical question (pp. 64-65)?
   a. What is the smallest difference in intensity that can be noticed?
   b. How do the qualities of the stimulus relate to qualities of our sensations and perceptions?
   c. What is the function of rods and cones in the retina?
   d. What is the least amount of a stimulus energy that can be detected?

2. Professor Zander wants to know how loud a certain noise must be in order to be heard from a distance of 50 feet. This question involves the concept of:
   a. relative magnitude.
   b. difference threshold.
   c. absolute threshold.
   d. inverse discrimination.

28

3. The aqueous humor is a fluid that carries nourishment to the cornea. It is recycled every four hours. A malfunction in this recycling system causes (pp. 65-66):
   a. cataracts.
   b. nearsightedness.
   c. farsightedness.
   d. glaucoma.

4. The "blind spot" of the eye refers to (p. 66):
   a. an area of the retina with no light receptors.
   b. an area of the retina taken up by the optic nerve.
   c. small areas of pigment in the eye peculiar to blind people.
   d. a and b above.

5. Seeing spots in front of your eyes can happen when (pp. 65-66):
   a. the cornea becomes pointed.
   b. impurities float through the aqueous humor.
   c. pressure builds up in the eye.
   d. cataracts develop in the lenses.

6. The "near point of accommodation" refers to (p. 66):
   a. a structure in the lens of the eye.
   b. the nearest point at which print can be read.
   c. the nearest point at which size constancy is possible.
   d. the nearest point at which figure can be distinguished from ground.

7. Which is *not* true about cones (p. 67)?
   a. They are located in the periphery.
   b. They are best for seeing detail.
   c. They are responsible for color vision.
   d. Each cone has its own bipolar cell.

8. "Unconscious inference theory" suggests that (p. 76):
   a. we correctly perceive the world because some aspect of the visual scene remains unchanged as other aspects change.
   b. ninety-nine percent of our perceptual judgments are totally unconscious.
   c. size constancy should not be possible.
   d. we unconsciously make accurate inferences about the world when given accurate information.

9. In following the visual pathways to the brain, light travels through various structures of the eye in which of the following orders (pp. 67-68)?
   a. ganglion cells, rods and cones, bipolar cells
   b. rods and cones, bipolar cells, ganglion cells
   c. bipolar cells, rods and cones, ganglion cells
   d. rods and cones, ganglion cells, bipolar cells

10. It takes approxiamtely _______________________ minutes for the eyes to adjust to a sharp
    decrease in the amount of light available (p. 69).
    a. 5
    b. 15
    c. 25
    d. 30

11. Once our eyes have adjusted to the current amount of light, our range of detection is from
    (p. 69):
    a. 10 times brighter to 10 times dimmer.
    b. 50 times brighter to 50 times dimmer.
    c. 100 times brighter to 100 times dimmer.
    d. 500 times brighter to 500 times dimmer.

12. Red-green color blindness (p. 69):
    a. causes individuals to see red and green as a light yellow.
    b. occurs in two out of 100 males.
    c. occurs in two out of 10,000 females.
    d. all of the above.

13. Which of the following is *not* true about trichromatic receptor theory (p. 73)?
    a. It was perfected by von Helmoltz.
    b. It explains color vision by positing three types of color receptors in the retina.
    c. It provides a good explanation for afterimages.
    d. It grew out of the work of Thomas Young, who conducted color mixture experiments.

14. Which of the following provides the best explanation for afterimages (p. 73)?
    a. opponent process theory
    b. image reversal theory
    c. dual process theory
    d. trichromatic receptor theory

15. Which of the following is *not* a Gestalt law of organization (p. 74)?
    a. law of proximity
    b. law of constant perception
    c. law of similarity
    d. law of figure/ground

16. One example of how we impose organization on stimuli, instead of simply taking sensory
    input "as is" is (p. 74):
    a. figure/ground reversal.
    b. multistable perception.
    c. a and b.
    d. neither a nor b.

17. When subjects view objects or people in a(n) ________________________, their judgments about size are inaccurate due to misleading information they have concerning the distance of those objects from themselves (p. 76).
    a. oscilloscope
    b. visual cliff apparatus
    c. distance-distortion room
    d. Ames room

18. The cue for depth perception that takes advantage of the fact that nearer elements are spaced farther apart than more distant elements is called (pp. 78-79):
    a. linear perspective.
    b. kinetic depth perception.
    c. the autokinetic effect.
    d. textural gradient.

19. Which of the following is *not* a monocular cue for depth perception (pp. 78-79)?
    a. disparity
    b. clearness
    c. linear perspective
    d. texture

20. Kraft and Elworth found that 16% of all airplane accidents are caused by (p. 79):
    a. visual illusions.
    b. malfunction of airplaine's instruments.
    c. pilot fatigue.
    d. figure/ground reversal.

21. The autokinetic effect (pp. 80-81):
    a. is the tendency for a stationary light to be viewed as moving.
    b. can be reduced by replacing single lights with clusters of lights.
    c. can be reduced by replacing stationary lights with flashing lights.
    d. all of the above.

22. The elastic flap that we normally refer to as the ear is called (p. 82):
    a. the basilar membrane.
    b. the oval window.
    c. the pinna.
    d. the earflap.

23. The inner ear contains the following structures:
    a. oval window and cochlea.
    b. oval window, cochlea, and ear canal.
    c. pinna and ear canal.
    d. eardrum and ear canal.

24. The eardrum, oval window, and basilar membrane have what characteristic in common
    (pp. 82-83)?
    a. They are all parts of the inner ear.
    b. They are all membranes.
    c. They all utilize bone conduction.
    d. They are all tubular passages.

25. When we listen to a high-quality tape recording of our voices, they sound odd to us because
    of (p. 83):
    a. bone conduction.
    b. air conduction.
    c. poor resolution.
    d. binaural disparity.

26. Which of the following is correct (pp. 83-84)?
    a. A change in pitch corresponds to a change in intensity of sound waves.
    b. Amplitude is measured using the unit "hertz."
    c. Frequency is measured using the unit "decibel."
    d. A change in pitch corresponds to a change in the frequency of sound waves.

27. Frequency theory (p. 84):
    a. states that we hear different pitches because different frequencies stimulate different places
        on the basilar membrane.
    b. states that receptors send pulses up the auditory nerve at the same frequency as the sound
        wave.
    c. explains how we hear sounds above 3,000 Hz.
    d. b and c above.

28. Wever's explanation that the combined response of different nerve fibers corresponds to the
    frequency of sound waves is called (p. 84):
    a. the combination principle.
    b. the vibration principle.
    c. the volley principle.
    d. the frequency principle.

29. If there is a disparity between the time a sound reaches one ear and the time it reaches the
    other ear (p. 86):
    a. the sound arrives later at the farther ear.
    b. the sound is louder at the farther ear.
    c. the sound phase is the same for both ears.
    d. the disparity is useless in locating the sound.

30. Taste buds (p. 87):
    a. are in direct contact with food.
    b. are never replaced if they die.
    c. are most sensitive between 22 and 32 degrees centigrade.
    d. are particularly sensitive in the elderly.

31. Assume you are 20 years old and in good health. Suppose you drink a glass of iced tea and it takes quite sour. This may be because (p. 87):
    a. the tea was sweetened when it was at room temperature.
    b. your taste buds have undergone "papillae desensitization."
    c. your sense of smell interferes with the taste.
    d. a large number of your taste buds have died since the tea was made.

32. Olfactory cells (p. 88):
    a. respond rapidly and are slow to fatigue.
    b. respond rapidly and fatigue rapidly.
    c. respond slowly but fatigue rapidly.
    d. none of the above.

33. When a warm object stimulates a cold spot on the skin, the result is called (p. 89):
    a. artificial warmth.
    b. paradoxical cold.
    c. warmth reversal.
    d. artificial cold.

34. Vascular theory (p. 89):
    a. is an attempt to explain pain perception.
    b. posits distinct receptors for the sensations of hot and cold.
    c. suggests that thermal receptors detect contraction and dilation of blood vessels.
    d. easily explains why we have hot and cold spots.

35. Which of the following structures is involved in our sense of equilibrium (p. 92)?
    a. vestibular system
    b. semicircular canals
    c. otolith structures
    d. all of the above

36. Motion sickness is caused by (p. 92):
    a. disagreements between auditory and vestibular information.
    b. disagreements between visual and vestibular information.
    c. disagreements between visual and auditory information.
    d. disagreements between auditory, visual, and vestibular information.

37. The function of the otolith structures is most similar to that of (p. 92):
    a. the eardrum.
    b. the basilar membrane.
    c. the cochlea.
    d. the semicircular canals.

38. In the Rock and Harris experiment concerning proprioception (pp. 92-93):
   a. wearing goggles that displace vision affected performance of *only* the practice arm.
   b. wearing goggles affected performance of *only* the rested arm.
   c. wearing goggles affected performance of *both* the practiced and rested arms.
   d. none of the above.

39. Hubel and Wiesel discovered that visual feature detectors of different complexities were neatly organized in the brain. One layer of cells, called complex cells, (p. 70):
   a. is responsible for detection of angles and other features.
   b. is responsible for detection of lines of specific orientation when they fall anywhere on the retina.
   c. is responsible for detection of circles and squares.
   d. none of the above.

40. The sonic guide (pp. 90-91):
   a. emits high-frequency sounds that are reflected back.
   b. gives the user electronic "music" that can be translated into information about the visual world.
   c. was used by a 16-month old baby to aid in reaching out to grasp objects.
   d. all of the above.

Answers to Practice Test

1. c	16. c	31. a
2. c	17. d	32. b
3. d	18. d	33. b
4. d	19. a	34. c
5. b	20. a	35. d
6. b	21. d	36. b
7. a	22. c	37. d
8. d	23. a	38. a
9. b	24. b	39. b
10. b	25. a	40. d
11. c	26. d	
12. d	27. b	
13. c	28. c	
14. a	29. a	
15. b	30. c	

THOUGHT QUESTIONS/APPLICATIONS

1. Much of the success of the Apollo 13 mission depended on the astronauts' abilities to interpret and use input from their senses. Discuss the various perceptual demands placed on the astronauts, using the following concepts from the chapter: absolute threshold, light and dark adaptation, monocular cues for depth perception, location of sounds, equilibrium, proprioception.

2. Suppose you are an artist and you are trying to represent two identical squares, one of which is further away than the other. Draw several pictures of the squares, using a different monocular cue for depth perception each time. Can you think of any cues besides the ones discussed in the chapter?

3. In your chapter, three "constancies" were discussed: size constancy, shape constancy, and brightness constancy. Can you think of any other constancies? What would your perceptual world be like if you didn't perceive constancies in your environment?

4. Obviously, the ability to localize sounds is essential in everyday activities. One way we localize sound is by relying on disparities between when a sound reaches one ear and when it reaches the other ear. However, when sounds are straight ahead, no such disparities exist. How do you distinguish between a sound that is straight ahead of you and another sound (of the same intensity and the same distance away) that is straight behind you?

Alternate States of Consciousness

CHAPTER OUTLINE

CHAPTER OBJECTIVES

After completing Chapter 4, you should:

1. Have an understanding of the term "consciousness," and understand what is meant by states of consciousness.

2. Know the two major viewpoints of altered states of consciousness, perceptual release and mysticism; and know how each attempts to explain these states.

3. Have an understanding of the different methods of studying states of consciousness.

4. Know that a state can be defined both in terms of physiological patterns and subjective patterns.

5. Be able to describe the physiological indices which define stages of sleep.

6. Know the various kinds of sleep disorders (insomnia and hypersomnia) and ways a clinician might treat these disorders.

7. Understand the relation between dreams and physiological patterns during sleep. What pysiological mechanism may be responsible for our "seeing" and "feeling" things during dreams?

8. Know the distinguishing characteristics of dreams, hypnagogic images, and daydreams.

9. Know the major types of psychoactive drugs and the physiological and subjective patterns associated with these drugs.

10. Know how hypnosis is defined, and know some of the situations in which it is used today.

11. Understand the nature of meditation, and its relation to the relaxation response and the flight-or-fight response.

12. Know how sensory deprivation is accomplished, and how people react to sensory deprivation.

13. Be able to describe how one might test a person for various types of extrasensory perception or psychokinesis.

KEY TERMS SELF-TEST

In each group below, fill in the letter of the term on the right with the appropriate definition on the left.

States of Consciousness

Definitions

Key Terms

_c_   1. the perception of what passes in one's own mind

_b_   2. mental states that differ in specific subjective and physiological patterns

_d_   3. the theory that the mind and brain are an organic whole

_a_   4. the theory that the mind and brain are separate entities

a. dualism (p. 102)
b. altered states of consciousnes (p. 100)
c. consciousness (p. 100)
d. monism (p. 102)

Sleep and Dreams

Definitions

Key Terms

_c_   1. the portion of the dream that a person remembers

_b_   2. the hidden content of dreams determined by unconscious impulses

_e_   3. stage of sleep marked by rapid eye movements

_a_   4. a sensory experience in the absence of external stimuli

_d_   5. hallucinations that occur during the drowsy interval before sleep

a. hallucinations (p. 113)
b. latent content (p. 108)
c. manifest content (p. 108)
d. hypnagogic images (p. 113)
e. REM sleep (p. 109)

Drugs, Hypnosis, and Meditation

Definitions

1. drugs that produce subjective effects

2. drugs that slow body functions

3. drugs that excite body functions

4. drugs that cause people to see visions and illusions

5. visual sensations arising from spontaneous discharges of neurons in the eye

6. a state of consciousness induced by the words and actions of a hypnotist

7. a state of consciousness in which the authority of the hypnotist is transferred to the individual

8. refers to the physiological patterns present during meditation

Key Terms

a. relaxation response (p. 126)
b. hallucinogens (p. 116)
c. hypnosis (p. 122)
d. stimulants (p. 116)
e. meditation (p. 124)
f. psychoactive drugs (p. 115)
g. phosphenes (p. 119)
h. depressants (p. 116)

Sensory Deprivation and Hidden Powers

Definitions

1. the absence of almost all sensory stimulation

2. the reception of information by means other than the usual senses

3. direct mental influence over physical objects

4. the perception of another's mental state by means of ESP

5. the perception of an object or event by means of ESP

6. perception of future thoughts, events, or actions.

Key Terms

a. telepathy (p. 129)
b. psychokinesis (p. 129)
c. sensory deprivation (p. 127)
d. precognition (p. 130)
e. clairvoyance (p. 130)
f. extrasensory perception (p. 129)

States of Consciousness
1. c
2. b
3. d
4. a

Sensory Deprivation and Hidden Powers
1. c   4. a
2. f   5. e
3. b   6. d

Sleep and Dreams
1. c
2. b
3. e
4. a
5. d

Drugs, Hypnosis, and Meditation
1. f   5. g
2. h   6. c
3. d   7. e
4. b   8. a

PRACTICE TEST

Circle the correct letter.

1. Which of the following should be used to define a particular state of consciousness (p. 100)?
   a. brain activity
   b. oxygen consumption
   c. sensations and thoughts
   d. all of the above

2. Which of the following viewpoints is characterized by the belief that the mind and brain are separate entities (p. 102)?
   a. monism
   b. dualism
   c. perceptual release theory
   d. mysticism

3. Different mental states with specific patterns of physiological and subjective responses are known as (p. 100):
   a. alternate states of consciousness.
   b. alternate states of conscience.
   c. dualism.
   d. drug-induced states only.

4. Which of the following viewpoints suggests that alternate states of consciousness are caused by an external reality (p. 102)?
   a. monism
   b. dualism
   c. perceptual release theory
   d. mysticism

5. Which of the following is not a method for studying alternate states of consciousness (pp. 103-104)?
   a. self-experience
   b. interviews
   c. method clinque
   d. All of the above can be used.

6. The reported experience from *Inside a Sioux Indian Sweat Lodge* demonstrates (p. 104):
   a. the role of hallucinogens in Indian ceremonies.
   b. the importance of focusing attention in producing certain altered states of consciousness.
   c. mind over matter.
   d. that mysticism is indeed the best explanation for the experiences in the sweat lodge.

7. The physiological patterns associated with near-death experiences indicate that (p. 105):
   a. there is a complete lapse in biological activity for an extended period of time.
   b. although breathing may be arrested, some heart and brain activities continue.
   c. some mechanism must be supplying the brain with oxygen and nourishment.
   d. none of the above.

8. Which of the following is *not* typically reported by people who have near-death experiences (p. 106)?
   a. meeting dead friends
   b. increased pain and anxiety
   c. the acquisition of new moral goals and determination
   d. hearing their doctor reporting them dead

9. According to Freud, the manifest content of a dream is (p. 108):
   a. what the dream was "really" about.
   b. that part of the dream that the dreamer remembers.
   c. that part of the dream determined by unconscious impulses.
   d. none of the above.

10. The latent content of dreams is (p. 108):
    a. what the dream was "really" about.
    b. that part of the dream that the dreamer remembers.
    c. that part of the dream determined by unconscious impulses.
    d. none of the above.

11. Stage two of sleep is characterized by ___________________ __________________, which are
    medium voltage, medium-frequency brain waves (p. 108).
    a. theta waves
    b. sleep spindles
    c. alpha waves
    d. delta waves

12. Stage _____________ sleep is referred to as REM sleep and is noted as the stage during which
    most dreams occur (p. 109).
    a. one
    b. three
    c. five
    d. six

13. When one goes for long periods of time without sleep, which of the following might be
    observed (p. 110)?
    a. increased stage two sleeping
    b. increased stage four sleeping
    c. REM rebound
    d. all of the above

14. Morpheus dreamed he was falling through a scary, dark well. This level of dreaming is called
    the (p. 110):
    a. reaction formation.
    b. libido.
    c. manifest content.
    d. latent content.

15. According to perceptual release theory, dreams are caused by (p. 112):
    a. the firing of giant cells in the brainstem.
    b. our fears and anxieties.
    c. stimulation from around us while we sleep.
    d. all of the above.

16. Sleep disorders such as insomnia are indicated by such things as (p. 111):
    a. the inability to sleep the night before an exam.
    b. not being able to regularly sleep at least eight hour a night.
    c. the inability to breathe properly during sleep.
    d. sleeplessness during temporary periods of depression.

17. Which of the following methods might not be useful in the treatment of sleep disorders
    (p. 111)?
    a. training a spouse of the client in identifying abnormal snoring patterns
    b. drug treatment
    c. biofeedback
    d. All of the above may be useful.

18. Seeing a gargoyle-type face would be a stage ________________ hypnagogic image (p. 113).
    a. one
    b. two
    c. three
    d. four

19. Visions during drowsiness should be distinguished from dreams because (p. 113):
    a. of their vivid content.
    b. they contain auditory images.
    c. they are in color instead of black and white.
    d. they occur during a transition stage between waking and sleeping.

20. Hypnagogic images are of a fixed pattern and (p. 113):
    a. do not occur in stages.
    b. occur during rapid eye movement.
    c. occur in a consistent sequence of four stages.
    d. occur following the onset of sleep spindles.

21. Unlike dreams, daydreams (p. 114):
    a. always are accompanied by a blank stare of the eyes.
    b. occur to everyone on a daily basis.
    c. are influenced by our daily activities.
    d. are not characterized by unique physiological patterns.

22. The amount of unhappy content of daydreams seems to be associated with (p. 115):
    a. insomnia.
    b. alcoholism.
    c. obesity.
    d. sexual conflict.

23. Depressants are *not* (pp. 116-117):
    a. vascular dilators.
    b. poisonous.
    c. physiologically addictive.
    d. psychologically addictive.

24. Which of the following is not a psychoactive drug (pp. 115-116)?
    a. caffeine
    b. alcohol
    c. nicotine
    d. All of the above *are* psychoactive drugs.

25. The effects of some psychoactive drugs can be influenced by (p. 116):
    a. cultural factors.
    b. personality.
    c. expectations of the drug user.
    d. all of the above.

26. Commonly used drugs include _______________________, which is a depressant, and

    _______________________, which is (are) a stimulant(s) (pp. 116-117).
    a. alcohol/caffeine
    b. speed/downers
    c. alcohol/nicotine
    d. cocaine/amphetamines

27. The subjective patterns associated with depressants include (p. 117):
    a. dilated pupils.
    b. a feeling of energy.
    c. release from social inhibitions.
    d. all of the above.

28. The physiological responses during LSD intoxication (p. 118):
    a. are similar to REM sleep.
    b. show a higher percentage of alpha brain waves.
    c. include hypertension.
    d. are similar to those of some stimulants.

29. Drug-induced hallucinations are characterized by (pp. 119-121):
    a. four stages of visual experiences.
    b. increased awareness of phosphenes.
    c. a progression from meaningless forms to more meaningful forms and then moving scenes.
    d. all of the above.

30. Hemophiliacs who do not bleed when their teeth are pulled are probably under the influence of (p. 122):
    a. hallucinogens.
    b. hypnagogens.
    c. hypnosis.
    d. stimulants.

31. The physiological patterns associated with hypnosis include (p. 122):
    a. altered blood flow to the brain.
    b. increased beta brain waves.
    c. decreased respiration rate.
    d. There are no consistent physiological patterns associated with hypnosis.

32. The subjective influences of hypnosis include influences on (p. 123):
    a. judgment and suggestibility.
    b. relaxation.
    c. attention and memory.
    d. all of the above.

33. Some of the "keys" to successful meditation include (pp. 124-125):
    a. sitting in an uncomfortable lotus position.
    b. trying to ignore your breathing patterns.
    c. regular daily practice (twice a day).
    d. all of the above.

34. Which of the following is *not* characteristic of the relaxation response resulting from meditation (p. 126)?
    a. decreased oxygen consumption
    b. lowered heart rate
    c. reduced muscle tension
    d. decreased alpha-wave levels

35. Sensory deprivation can lead to (p. 128):
    a. hallucinations.
    b. reduced arithmetic performance.
    c. increased scores on IQ tests.
    d. all of the above.

36. Which of the following forms of hidden mental powers would include the ability to perceive another's mental state (pp. 129-130)?
    a. telepathy
    b. clairvoyance
    c. precognition
    d. psychokinesis

37. Which of the following forms of hidden mental powers would include the ability to perceive an object or event by means of ESP (pp. 129-130)?
    a. telepathy
    b. clairvoyance
    c. precognition
    d. psychokinesis

1. d	16. c	31. d
2. b	17. d	32. d
3. a	18. c	33. c
4. d	19. d	34. d
5. c	20. c	35. d
6. b	21. d	36. a
7. c	22. b	37. b
8. b	23. a	
9. b	24. d	
10. c	25. d	
11. b	26. a	
12. b	27. c	
13. c	28. a	
14. c	29. d	
15. d	30. c	

THOUGHT QUESTIONS/APPLICATIONS

1. Consider the definition of states of consciousness. Can you think of any states of consciousness that were not discussed in the text? What would the physiological and subjective patterns of one such state be?

2. Consider the subjective and physiological patterns associated with daydreaming and meditation. How are these two states different? How are they the same?

3. Try to remember your most recent dream. Write a description of the manifest content of the dream. Now analyze the dream for possible latent content.

4. Do you think that watching television induces an altered state of consciousness? Why or why not?

5

Learning and Intelligence

CHAPTER OUTLINE

CHAPTER OBJECTIVES

After completing Chapter 5, you should:

1. Have an understanding of the definition of learning.

2. Know the historical roots of classical conditioning.

3. Be able to label the components of a classical conditioning procedure with the terms: CS, CR, US, and UR.

4. Be able to identify several important factors which influence the acquisition and maintenance of classically conditioned responses.

5. Know the differences between classical conditioning and operant conditioning.

6. Understand the role of reinforcement in operant conditioning and the effects of various schedules of reinforcement.

7. Understand the differences among positive reinforcement, negative reinforcement, and punishment.

8. Know several ways one might encourage a first operant response.

9. Know how to decrease the frequency of an operant response through extinction or punishment.

10. Understand why some responses may be more easily learned than others for a given organism.

11. Know what latent learning is and why it is important for cognitive theories of learning.

12. Know how a learning set may facilitate problem solving, while a negative set may make it hard to see a simple solution to a problem.

13. Understand the complex nature of measuring intelligence, and know the possible subdivisions of intelligence into fluid intelligence and crystallized intelligence.

14. Know some of the controversies surrounding the use of intelligence tests to subdivide people into different intelligence levels.

KEY TERMS SELF-TEST

In each group below, fill in the letter of the term on the right with the appropriate definition on the left.

Definition of Learning, Classical Conditioning

Definitions

Key Terms

1. process by which experience results in a relatively permanent change in potential behavior

2. process by which an original neutral stimulus comes to elicit a response that was originally given to another stimulus

a. extinction (p. 142)
b. classical conditioning (p. 139)
c. spontaneous recovery (p. 142)
d. learning (p. 138)
e. discrimination (p. 143)
f. stimulus generalization (p. 143)
g. latent learning (p. 138)

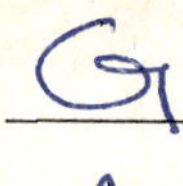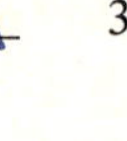

_G_   3. learning that does not show itself immediately in performance

_A_   4. gradual falling off in a response when the CS is repeatedly presented alone

_C_   5. when an extinguished response reappears without any retraining

_F_   6. when responses are made to stimuli similar to, but not the same as the original stimulus

_E_   7. when one learns to respond only to specific stimuli and not to other similar stimuli

Operant Conditioning

Definitions

_E_   1. an event whose occurrence just after a response increases the likelihood that the response will be repeated

_B_   2. when a positive stimulus is added to the environment and has a reinforcing effect

_C_   3. when a stimulus is taken away or stopped and this has a reinforcing effect

_F_   4. a stimulus that decreases the likelihood of a response when it is added to the environment

_D G_   5. events that are reinforcing only after they have been paired with primary reinforcers

_D_   6. when a subject receives a reinforcer for every correct response

_A_   7. when a subject is reinforced every few responses or every once in awhile

Key Terms

a. partial reinforcement (p. 147)
b. positive reinforcement (p. 146)
c. negative reinforcement (p. 146)
d. continuous reinforcement (p. 147)
e. reinforcement (p. 144)
f. punishment (p. 152)
g. secondary reinforcers (p. 146)

Operant Conditioning, Cognitive Learning Theory

Definitions

1. when parts of a behavior are reinforced until the whole desired behavior is learned

2. the idea that animals are more prepared to make certain responses than others

3. a mental picture of a maze or other surrounding environment

4. when a previous experience makes one ready to solve a particular type of problem

5. difficulty in the learning of new uses of something that has served a specific function in the past

Key Terms

a. cognitive map (p. 159)
b. preparedness (p. 156)
c. learning set (p. 160)
d. shaping (p. 150)
e. functional fixedness (p. 161)

Intelligence

Definitions

1. a test designed to measure a person's current knowledge and skills

2. a test designed to predict capacity for future performance

3. mental age divided by chronoloical age and multiplied by 100

4. general mental skills, such as the ability to make inferences

5. specific mental skills, such as one's vocabulary

Key Terms

a. Intelligence Quotient (p. 163)
b. crystallized intelligence (p. 165)
c. achievement tests (p. 162)
d. fluid intelligence (p. 164)
e. aptitude tests (p. 162)

Answers to Key Terms Self-Test

Definition of Learning, Classical Conditioning

1. d   5. c
2. b   6. f
3. g   7. e
4. a

Operant Conditioning

1. e   5. g
2. b   6. d
3. c   7. a

Operant Conditioning, Cognitive Learning Theory

Intelligence

1. d

1. c

2. b

2. e

3. a

3. a

4. c

4. d

5. e

5. b

PRACTICE TEST

Circle the correct letter.

1. The process by which experience or practice results in a relatively permanent change in behavior is called (p. 138):
   a. learning
   b. latent learning
   c. intelligence gain
   d. conditioning

2. The concept of latent learning recognizes the difference between ________________

   and ________________ (p. 138).
   a. classical conditioning/operant conditioning
   b. nature/nurture
   c. learning/performance
   d. conditioned response/unconditioned response

3. The process by which an originally neutral stimulus comes to elicit a response is called (p. 139):
   a. conditional learning.
   b. classical conditioning.
   c. instrumental conditioning.
   d. operant conditioning.

4. Pavlov won the Nobel prize for his research in (pp. 138-139):
   a. classical conditioning.
   b. digestion.
   c. reflex behavior.
   d. operant conditioning.

5. When Pavlov trained his dogs to salivate in response to a bell, the food served as the (pp. 139-140):
   a. US
   b. CS
   c. UR
   d. CR

6. When Pavlov trained his dogs to salivate in response to a bell, the salivation in response to the bell alone was called (pp. 139-140):
   a. US
   b. CS
   c. UR
   d. CR

7. If one were to train an alcoholic to avoid alcohol through the use of a drug that causes vomiting, the CS would be (p. 142):
   a. the drug.
   b. vomiting.
   c. the smell or taste of alcohol.
   d. none of the above.

8. Which of the following would *not* be important in establishing a response in classical conditioning (pp. 140-142)?
   a. a distinctive CS
   b. a strong CR
   c. the order of the CS and US
   d. the time between the CS and US

9. Fido tended to barely wag his tail every time before he jumped up on Lucy, scaring her and causing her to cry. Tail wagging probably did not become a CS because (pp. 140-141):
   a. there were not enough repeated pairings between US and CS.
   b. the CS was not distinctive enough.
   c. there was too great a tme lapse between CS and US.
   d. the US occurred before the CS.

10. The decrease in strength of the CR as a result of repeated pairings of the CS *alone* is called (p. 142):
    a. extinction.
    b. spontaneous recovery.
    c. higher order conditioning.
    d. discrimination.

11. When a CS is presented several days after extinction, the CR may reappear. This is called (p. 142):
    a. secondary extinction.
    b. generalization.
    c. spontaneous recovery.
    d. disinhibition.

12. Albert was classically conditioned to fear a white rat. He was then afraid of a white rabbit, a fur coat, and Santa Claus. This example illustrates (p. 142):
    a. stimulus generalization.
    b. response generalization.
    c. discrimination.
    d. all of the above.

13. Stimulus discrimination (p. 143):
    a. is a response followed by a reinforcer.
    b. occurs when responses are made to stimuli that are similar to the original CS.
    c. is the removal of a stimulus.
    d. occurs when responses are made to certain stimuli, but not to others.

14. When a well-established CS is paired with another CS, a response can be learned to the second CS without presentation of the US. This is called (p. 143):
    a. discrimination.
    b. stimulus generalization.
    c. higher order conditioning.
    d. operant conditioning.

15. According to Thorndike, animals tend to repeat behaviors that are followed by "good effects." This relation is called (p. 144):
    a. operant conditioning.
    b. law of use.
    c. reinforcement.
    d. law of effect.

16. Thorndike taught cats to pull a cord to get out of a cage to reach a small bowl of food. In this example, the food is (p. 144):
    a. the reinforcement.
    b. the operant.
    c. the response.
    d. the motivating force.

17. A rat can learn to press a lever to turn off a shock. This is an example of (p. 146):
    a. avoidance training.
    b. negative reinforcement.
    c. punishment training.
    d. positive reinforcement.

18. If a rat can press a lever prior to being shocked, and thus avoid the shock, the procedure would be an example of (p. 146):
    a. avoidance training.
    b. escape training.
    c. punishment training.
    d. positive reinforcement.

19. If a rat continues to press a bar in a Skinner box when the response only turns on a light, then the light has become a (p. 146):
   a. primary reinforcer.
   b. secondary reinforcer.
   c. partial reinforcer.
   d. generalized reinforcer.

20. Suppose you have six chores you are to do each week. You will receive your allowance when you have completed your chores. Your allowance is given to you on a _____________________ reinforcement schedule (pp. 146-147):
   a. continuous
   b. fixed interval
   c. fixed ratio
   d. variable interval

21. Which of the following schedules of reinforcement produces the most inconsistent response rate (pp. 147-148)?
   a. variable ratio
   b. fixed ratio
   c. fixed interval
   d. variable interval

22. Your mail is delivered everyday at around 10:00 a.m. However, some days it is delivered early, and some days it is late. This is an example of a _____________________ reinforcement schedule (pp. 146-147).
   a. variable ratio
   b. variable interval
   c. fixed interval
   d. fixed ratio

23. Which of the following is *not* a method to encourage the acquisition of an operant response (p. 149)?
   a. increased motivation
   b. modeling
   c. shaping
   d. All of the above *are* methods of encouraging an operant response.

24. _____________________ decreases the likelihood of a response when it is *added* to an environment (p. 152).
   a. Extinction
   b. Punishment
   c. Negative reinforcement
   d. All of the above have the effect.

25. If a child says "da-da" in response to his/her father, and also to other men, the child is showing (pp. 154-155):
   a. stimulus generalization.
   b. response generalization.
   c. discrimination.
   d. spontaneous recovery.

26. Which of the following is not an application of operant conditioning (pp. 154-155)?
   a. token economies
   b. programmed instruction
   c. relaxation training with biofeedback
   d. All of the above are possible applications.

27. Rats learn to jump to avoid a shock faster than they learn to press a bar to avoid the same shock. This is an example of (p. 156):
   a. punishment.
   b. preparedness.
   c. cognitive learning.
   d. all of the above.

28. The concept of preparedness in operant learning included all but which one of the following concepts (p. 156)?
   a. intelligence
   b. physique
   c. prior learning
   d. equality of subjects

29. Köhler argues that chimpanzees learned through ___________________, a process which should be contrasted with _______________ methods of learning observed in Thorndike's cats (p. 158).
   a. operant conditioning/classical conditioning
   b. classical conditioning/operant conditioning
   c. trial and error/insight
   d. insight/trial and error

30. Tolman demonstrated that rats learned their way around a maze even when they were not reinforced for making correct turns. This is an example of (pp. 158-159):
   a. insight.
   b. latent learning.
   c. a learning set.
   d. clairvoyance.

31. Tolman argued that rats learn a mental picture of the maze used in his studies. He called this a (p. 159):
    a. mental image.
    b. mental set.
    c. cognitive map.
    d. functional fixedness.

32. If you solve a series of water jar problems, all with the same, complex solution then (p. 161):
    a. you would find it easy to solve a water jar problem with a different, simpler solution.
    b. you would find it easy to solve a water jar problem with the same kind of solution.
    c. you would have trouble solving a water jar problem with a different, simpler solution.
    d. b and c above.

33. People have difficulty discovering solutions to problems that require the use of tools in ways differing from the usual usage. This is called (p. 161):
    a. learning set.
    b. functional fixedness.
    c. mental set.
    d. negative set.

34. Psychologists recognize the difference between opportunity to learn and capacity to learn by distinguishing between (p. 162):
    a. achievement tests and aptitude tests.
    b. mental age and chronological age.
    c. intelligence and performance.
    d. nature and nurture.

35. The average performance of children at a specific chronological age is called (p. 163):
    a. chronological age.
    b. intelligence quotient.
    c. mental age.
    d. standardized test performance.

36. _________________________________ is defined by the formula:
    (Mental Age/Chronological Age) $\times$ 100 (p. 163).
    a. Fluid intelligence
    b. Aptitude
    c. Both a and be are.
    d. Intelligence quotient

37. The decline in IQ scores after the age of forty may be due to (pp. 164-165):
    a. a decline in fluid intelligence.
    b. a decline in crystallized intelligence.
    c. cultural biases of the IQ test.
    d. none of the above; IQ does not start declining at age 40.

38. The lack of exposure of some groups of a society to material covered on IQ tests suggests that the IQ test may lack (pp. 166-167):
 a. cultural fairness.
 b. internal validity.
 c. an ability to predict future performance.
 d. all of the above.

39. Studies of adopted children which compare their IQs to those of both their biological and adopted parents indicated (p. 168):
 a. that nurture is more important than nature.
 b. the IQ correlation between parent and biological child is higher than between parent and adopted child.
 c. the IQ correlation between genetically related brothers and sisters is not consistently higher than between brothers and sisters by adoption.
 d. a and b.

40. The study of the IQ of different races indicates that (p. 169):
 a. minority groups often score lower on IQ tests than white people.
 b. blacks are innately less intelligent than whites.
 c. IQ differences can be attributed entirely to genetic differences between the races.
 d. a and b above.

Answers to Practice Test

1. a	16. a	31. c
2. c	17. b	32. d
3. b	18. a	33. b
4. b	19. b	34. a
5. a	20. c	35. c
6. d	21. c	36. d
7. c	22. b	37. a
8. b	23. d	38. a
9. b	24. b	39. c
10. a	25. a	40. a
11. c	26. d	
12. a	27. b	
13. d	28. d	
14. c	29. d	
15. d	30. b	

1. John is an avid chewing gum chewer. In fact, every time he saw a pack of gum he would salivate. What kind of conditioning is this? Identify the relevant components (for example, the US, CS, etc., or the reinforcement, etc.).

2. Design an operant conditioning procedure to increase your use of this study guide. What schedule of reinforcement should you use?

3. Consider the following procedure. A rat is put in a box with an electric grid on the floor. Two seconds before the rat is shocked, a red light goes on. The rat can avoid the shock by jumping to the other side of the box. After several learning trials, the rat learns to jump to the other side of the box in response to the red light. Analyze this situation in terms of *both* operant conditioning and classical conditioning. How can we decide which interpretation is correct?

4. Consider the problem of cultural biases of standard IQ tests. How could one devise a "culturally bias free" IQ test? Think of some of your own questions to be included on such a test.

6

Memory and Cognition

CHAPTER OUTLINE

CHAPTER OBJECTIVES

After completing Chapter 6, you should:

1. Know several different methods of testing memory and that different methods may lead to different levels of performance.

2. Understand that memory can be divided into three types: sensory memory, short-term memory, and long-term memory.

3. Know the difference between the multiple storage theory of memory and the levels of processing theory of memory.

4. Know the different characteristics of short-term memory and long-term memory in terms of capacity and forgetting.

5. Understand the limited nature of attention and how attention is studied using "shadowing" tasks in the laboratory.

6. Be able to give examples of verbal codes and visual codes in memory.

7. Understand what is meant by the term encode and know how encoding may affect both how well we remember and what we remember.

8. Know the relation between memory span and chunking and the importance of 7 ± 2.

9. Understand that long-term memory is organized, and know how this organization affects our memory.

10. Know that information in short-term memory and long-term memory must be retrieved and how retieval cues, anxiety, and decision factors may influence retrieval processes.

11. Be able to describe the two major theories of foregetting and how one measures two different types of interference.

12. Be able to describe the key-word method of learning foreign vocabulary.

13. Know how to improve your memory by encoding reading material more efficiently.

14. Know how to best review material for an upcoming test.

KEY TERMS SELF-TEST

In each group below, fill in the letter of the term on the right with the appropriate definition on the left.

Measuring Memory

Definitions

Key Terms

 1. a system that allows people to retain information over time

 2. a test that measures a person's ability to reproduce material with or without retrieval cues

 3. a test that measures a person's ability to pick the correct answer when several answers are given

a. recognition test (p. 177)
b. free association test (p. 188)
c. memory (p. 176)
d. recall test (p. 177)
e. savings test (p. 177)

_____ 4. a measure of a person's ability to take advantage of poor learning to relearn material

_____ 5. a test in which a person is given a target word and is asked to report other words that come to mind

Types of Memory

Definitions

Key Terms

 1. holds sensations briefly so that they can be identified

 2. process of repeating information in order to retain it

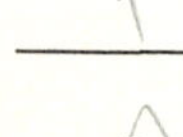 3. holds information that is transferred from short-term memory

a. memory span (p. 186)
b. chunking (p. 186)
c. semantic memory (p. 187)
d. rehearsal (p. 180)
e. sensory memory (p. 178)
f. long-term memory (p. 181)
g. episodic memory (p. 187)

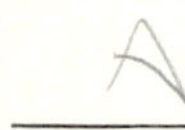 4. the number of items that we can read through one time and then recall in sequence with no errors

5. process of grouping items into units
that function as wholes in memory

6. memories about events, including
time and place

7. general background knowledge about
words, concepts, and rules

Loss of Memory

Definitions

1. paying mind to important stimuli
and ignoring irrelevant ones

2. aids to the recovery of information
stored in memory

3. a state of being on the verge of
recalling something

4. an inability to remember or retrieve
information from memory

5. theory that memories fade away
with time

6. theory that we forget information
because other information gets in
the way

Key Terms

a. tip-of-the-tongue (p. 194)
b. trace decay (p. 196)
c. foregetting (p. 196)
d. retrieval cues (p. 193)
e. interference (p. 197)
f. attention (p. 182)

Memory Aids

Definitions

1. interference of previous learning
with memory for new material

2. interference of new learning with
memory for previously learned
material

3. systems created to aid memory

4. system of using imagery to learn
foreign vocabulary

5. system of relating new material to
words that are easy to remember

Key Terms

a. verbal mediation (p. 201)
b. retroactive inhibition (p. 197)
c. mnemonics (p. 200)
d. key-word method (p. 200)
e. proactive inhibition (p. 197)

Measuring Memory

1. c   4. e
2. d   5. b
3. a

Types of Memory

1. e   5. b
2. d   6. g
3. f   7. c
4. a

Loss of Memory

1. f   4. c
2. d   5. b
3. a   6. e

Memory Aids

1. c   4. d
2. b   5. a
3. c

PRACTICE TEST

Circle the correct letter.

1. A mental framework such as "One is bun, two is shoe. . . ." is called a (p. 176):
   a. program.
   b. schemata.
   c. image.
   d. memory.

2. A test that measures a person's ability to reproduce material in any order is called a

   _________________ test (p. 177).
   a. cued recall
   b. free recall
   c. recognition
   d. savings

3. A test that measures a person's ability to take advantage of what one has learned before in order to relearn material faster is called (p. 177):
   a. cued recall.
   b. free recall.
   c. recognition.
   d. savings.

4. The two theories of memory are the multiple memory theory and the (p. 178):
   a. dual-process theory.
   b. short-term memory theory.
   c. levels of processing theory.
   d. partial report theory.

5. The two theories of memory disagree about the number of memory stores, but they agree
   about (p. 178):
   a. the existence of sensory memory.
   b. the role of rehearsal.
   c. the existence of short-term memory.
   d. all of the above.

6. When studying sensory memory, Sperling found that (pp. 178-179):
   a. subjects could report more from a visual display with partial report than when they
      were asked to report the whole display.
   b. subjects reported more from the visual display than they could see.
   c. the estimate of how much subjects saw in the display based on partial report was greater
      than the amount of information subjects could report when asked to report the whole
      display.
   d. a tone following a visual display caused backward masking.

7. Which of the following is not a property of sensory memory (p. 180)?
   a. Visual properties of the stimulus determine the length of sensory memory.
   b. One stimulus is wiped out when another stimulus is presented after the first one is out
      of sight.
   c. It has a limit to the amount of information it can hold; the limit is 7 ± 2 chunks of
      information.
   d. It contains information that has not yet been recognized or named.

8. Information in short-term memory is lost or forgotten if it is not rehearsed in about
   (p. 180):
   a. 15 seconds.
   b. 30 seconds.
   c. 30 minutes.
   d. 2 seconds.

9. The longer that information stays in short-term memory, the more likely it is to be (p. 181):
   a. forgotten.
   b. subject to backward masking.
   c. transferred to long-term memory.
   d. attended to.

10. Information that is transferred from short-term memory through rehearsal or some other
    process is probably now in (p. 181):
    a. sensory memory.
    b. long-term memory.
    c. rehearsal.
    d. visual memory.

11. Seven minutes after reading a sentence you will probably remember (p. 185):
   a. sentence meaning but not the exact wording of the sentence.
   b. the exact wording of the sentence.
   c. very little about the sentence unless the exact wording of the sentence has been transferred to long-term memory.
   d. all of the above.

12. A special plan to represent information in memory is called (p. 182):
   a. decoding.
   b. encoding.
   c. attention.
   d. depth of processing.

13. Recognition processes operate in spite of disruptions because of (p. 178):
   a. cued recall.
   b. savings.
   c. long-term memory.
   d. sensory memory.

14. In the laboratory investigation of attention, subjects are asked to ignore information presented in one ear and to _______________ the other message.
   a. ignore
   b. memorize
   c. encode
   d. shadow

15. In an attention experiment, which of the following information would a subject remember about the irrelevant message 30 seconds after presentation (p. 183)?
   a. changes in languages
   b. the meaning of the message
   c. changes from a male's to a female's voice
   d. all of the above

16. When trying to recall a list of letters, people often incorrectly recall a letter that sounds like a correct letter. This is evidence that people are remembering a (p. 184):
   a. verbal code.
   b. sensory images.
   c. visual code.
   d. visual image.

17. The number of items that we can read through one time and then recall in sequence with no mistakes is called (p. 186):
   a. real memory.
   b. free recall.
   c. semantic memory.
   d. memory span.

18. The "magical" number 7 ± 2 refers to the limited number of _________________ that we
can retain in short-term memory (p. 186).
a. items
b. chunks
c. words
d. ideas

19. Which of the following groups of items would be hardest to retain (p. 186)?
a. 555-1213
b. December 7, 1941
c. George Washington
d. X N 9 W F 4

20. _________________ _________________ refers to a person's general background
knowledge about words, symbols, concepts, and rules (p. 187).
a. Episodic memory
b. Hierarchical memory
c. Semantic memory
d. Short-term memory

21. People often recall lists of words not in their original order, but in related groups. This result
shows the effects of _________________ _________________ on _________________
_________________ (p. 188).
a. semantic memory/episodic memory
b. episodic memory/semantic memory
c. encoding/retrieval
d. free association/long-term memory

22. Memory for an event is often altered to include details of the event that did not actually exist.
This is an example of (p. 191):
a. retrieval failure.
b. reconstructive memory.
c. forgetting.
d. all of the above.

23. Which of the following is probably a leading question with regard to whether or not the burglar
in a crime had a beard (p. 191)?
a. Did you notice anything on the burglar's face?
b. What did the suspect look like?
c. How much of the burglar's face was covered by his beard?
d. Did the burglar have a beard?

24. The process of getting information out of memory is called (p. 192):
    a. retrieval.
    b. recall.
    c. reconstruction.
    d. all of the above.

25. Memorize the numbers 2, 3, and 8. Is the number 3 on this list? This task is an example of (p. 192):
    a. iconic memory.
    b. retrieval from short-term memory.
    c. retrieval from long-term memory.
    d. tip-of-the-tongue.

26. Category names can serve as aids when one is trying to remember words on a list. These aids are called (p. 193):
    a. retrieval cues.
    b. TOTs.
    c. hints.
    d. memory traces.

27. The uncomfortable state of being on the verge of recalling something is called (p. 194):
    a. tip-of-the-tongue.
    b. repression.
    c. amnesia.
    d. retrieval.

28. High anxiety can cause a person to do poorly on an exam because (pp. 194-195):
    a. anxiety causes repression.
    b. anxiety prevents retrieval.
    c. anxiety produces extraneous thoughts which interfere with retrieval of test answers.
    d. anxiety wipes out memory.

29. In terms of decision processes in memory, a "hit" is (p. 196):
    a. a "yes" to a true statement.
    b. a "no" to a false statement.
    c. a "yes" to a false statement.
    d. a and b above.

30. According to trace-decay theory, we forget because (pp. 196-197):
    a. of interference of previous learning with memory for the new.
    b. memory becomes weak from disuse.
    c. of interference of new learning with memory for old.
    d. traces strengthen over time.

31. A popular theory of forgetting holds that we forget information because other information gets in the way. This theory is called (p. 197):
    a. trace-decay theory.
    b. proactive interference.
    c. interference theory.
    d. retrieval-failure theory.

32. Interference of previous learning with memory for new learning is called (p. 197):
    a. proactive inhibition.
    b. decay.
    c. retroactive inhibition.
    d. retroactive amnesia.

33. Compare groups one and two below. This comparison provides a means to evaluate (pp. 197-198):
> *Group 1:* learn list a, learn list b, recall list b.
> *Group 2:* rest, learn list b, recall list b.
    a. forgetting.
    b. proactive inhibition.
    c. retroactive inhibition.
    d. nonspecific transfer.

34. You can improve your memory for names if during an introduction to a person you ask yourself if there is anything unusual about the name. This is an example of what type of memory aid (pp. 198-199)?
    a. retrieval cue.
    b. efficient review.
    c. efficient encoding.
    d. visual imagery.

35. Memory-aiding systems are called (p. 200):
    a. verbal mediators.
    b. depth of processing.
    c. muleta.
    d. mnemonic systems.

36. In the key-word method of learning a foreign vocabulary, one makes use of ____________________ to help them learn the terms (p. 200).
    a. imagery
    b. verbal mediators
    c. rehearsal
    d. depth of processing

37. Students who have learned the Great Lakes by remembering the word HOMES are using a memory-aid called (p. 201):
    a. key-word method.
    b. verbal mediation.
    c. organization.
    d. depth of processing.

38. Thinking up test questions and criticizing the text aids in memory retention by increasing one's (pp. 201-202):
    a. organization.
    b. depth of processing.
    c. intelligence.
    d. trace decay.

39. Trying to establish the context in which you learned some information may help you remember the information by helping you (p. 202):
    a. organize the information.
    b. increase depth of processing.
    c. search your memory systematically.
    d. all of the above.

40. A computer can help improve eyewitness memory by (p. 203):
    a. reducing the number of faces the eyewitness has to search through.
    b. automatically selecting features which discriminate between a subset of photos.
    c. allowing the witness to rate features such as "business of eyebrows" on a numerical scale.
    d. all of the above.

1. b		21. a	
2. b		22. b	
3. d		23. c	
4. c		24. a	
5. a		25. b	
6. c		26. a	
7. c		27. a	
8. b		28. c	
9. c		29. a	
10. b		30. b	
11. a		31. c	
12. b		32. a	
13. d		33. b	
14. d		34. c	
15. c		35. d	
16. a		36. a	
17. d		37. b	
18. b		38. b	
19. d		39. c	
20. c		40. d	

THOUGHT QUESTIONS/APPLICATIONS

1. A number of different memory aids outlined in this chapter involved the use of visual imagery. Why do you think forming an image of a word would make that word easier to remember?

2. The different measures of memory (e.g., recall, cued recall, recognition, and savings) all yield different estimates of the amount of material one retains. What does this suggest about learning and memory processes? How can we (or can we) get a pure measure of the amount retained?

3. Consider the phenomenon of state dependent memory. What does it suggest concerning how one should study for a test.

4. Suppose you have two exams on the same day. How should you divide your study time on the day before the exams? Which exam should you study for first? Discuss your answer in terms of short-term memory, long-term memory, and interference.

Infancy and Childhood

CHAPTER OUTLINE

CHAPTER OBJECTIVES

After completing Chapter 7, you should:

1. See why Genie's abnormal development was influenced by both genetic and environmental factors.

2. Be able to weigh the advantages and disadvantages of longitudinal and cross-sectional approaches and see why neither is the "perfect" developmental method of research.

3. Be able to explain why critical periods cannot be explained by either the "nativism" or the "empiricism" theories.

4. Know the highlights of the three stages of prenatal development (Period of the Ovum, Period of the Embryo, Period of the Fetus).

5. Be acutely aware that women should be concerned about the welfare of their infants long before they are born and should carefully control their exposure to diseases, drugs, radiation, and so forth.

6. Have a general grasp of the normal course of physical growth and be able to use that knowledge as a "yardstick" for judging what is normal and abnormal.

7. Realize that the obvious physical differences between infants and older children are mirrored by much more subtle differences in the nervous system.

8. Know that infants come into the world with a large repertoire of reflexes and that these reflexes vary in both appearance and function.

9. See that motor development progresses from simple reflexes to voluntary control of the body's movement.

10. Be able to argue that the world is *not* a "blooming, buzzing confusion" for the young infant. Instead, the infant can perceive size and depth, and even has certain visual "preferences."

11. Be able to describe, in terms of Piaget's theory of development, exactly how children are "different" from adults in their thinking.

12. Know the highlights of each of the four stages of development in Piaget's theory.

13. Understand why imitation and operant conditioning cannot possibly explain all aspects of language development.

14. Be able to answer the question of whether chimps can learn human language.

15. See why simply providing nutrition is *not* enough to insure the attachment of the young organism to his or her mother.

16. Know why some children become securely attached to their mothers while others become anxiously attached.

17. Be able to compare and contrast the roles of parents, teachers, and peers in the child's development.

In each group below, fill in the letter of the term on the right with the appropriate definition on the left.

Studying Development

Definitions

Key Terms

1. process by which genes come to be expressed as specific physical and behavioral characteristics

2. research in which the same person or group is tested over a period of time

3. research in which people of different ages are tested at the same period of time

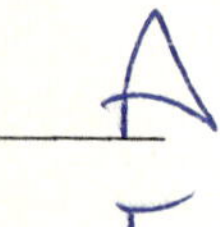

4. the unfolding of genetically determined abilities

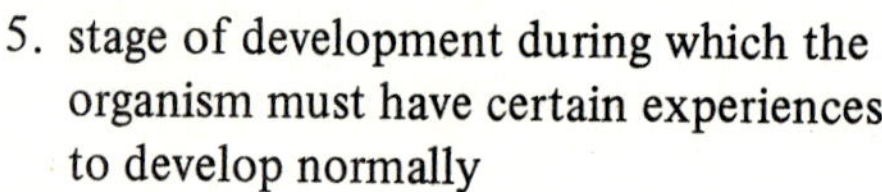

5. stage of development during which the organism must have certain experiences to develop normally

a. maturation (p. 211)
b. cross-sectional research (p. 210)
c. longitudinal research (p. 210)
d. development (p. 210)
e. critical period (p. 211)

Prenatal Development

Definitions

Key Terms

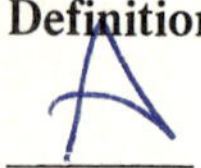

1. term describing the human organism during the first two weeks of prenatal development

2. term describing the human organism from the third week through the eighth week in the uterus

3. term describing the human organism from the third month through to the time of birth

a. ovum (p. 212)
b. placenta (p. 212)
c. embryo (212)
d. Apgar scoring system (p. 215)
e. fetus (p. 212)

4. filter used to exchange food and wastes between an embryo and his or her mother

5. scale used to assess the condition of newborns

Birth to 1 Year

Definitions

1. development of myelin sheaths during infancy, childhood, and adolescence

2. automatic action that requires no conscious effort

3. reflex causing infants to turn their heads toward anything that touches cheek

4. reflex causing infants to prance in a "tip-toe" motion when held upright with feet touching a surface

5. reflex causing a motor reaction of arms, legs, and trunk in response to a sudden loud noise or loss of support

6. reflex causing infants on their backs to move their arms and legs into a "fencing" position when the head is turned to one side

7. apparatus used to test depth perception in infants

Key Terms

a. rooting reflex (p. 217)
b. tonic neck reflex (p. 217)
c. reflex (p. 217)
d. myelinization (p. 217)
e. dancing reflex (p. 217)
f. visual cliff (p. 219)
g. Moro or startle reflex (p. 217)

Childhood

Definitions

1. term used to refer to a mental structure that organizes responses to experiences

2. process of interpreting events in a way that fits existing ideas or schema

Key Terms

a. assimilation (p. 223)
b. attachment (p. 231)
c. imprinting (p. 233)
d. accommodation (p. 223)
e. schema (p. 222)
f. identification (p. 233)
g. holophrastic speech (p. 227)

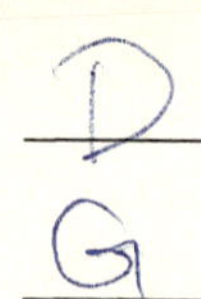

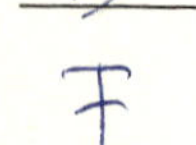

_____ 3. process of adjusting one's schema to fit environmental demands

_____ 4. use of a single word to express phrases

_____ 5. tendency of children to seek closeness to certain people

_____ 6. process of acquiring personality and social behaviors by taking on characteristics of others

_____ 7. attachment formed by duckling for almost any moving object that it first sees

Answers to Key Terms Self-Test

Studying Development

1. d	4. a
2. c	5. e
3. b	

Prenatal Development

1. a	4. b
2. c	5. d
3. e	

Birth to 1 Year

1. d	5. g
2. c	6. b
3. a	7. f
4. e	

Childhood

1. e	5. b
2. a	6. f
3. d	7. c
4. g	

PRACTICE TEST

Circle the correct letter.

1. Development is controlled by (p. 210):
   a. heredity.
   b. environment.
   c. a continuous interaction between heredity and environment.
   d. none of the above.

2. Longitudinal research (p. 210):
   a. is an approach in which the responses of different people of different ages are compared.
   b. permits researchers to look at stability of behavior.
   c. is an approach in which the same person or group is tested over a period of time.
   d. b and c above.

3. A major *disadvantage* of cross-sectional research is (pp. 210-211):
   a. that cultural and historical experiences are difficult to control across people of different ages.
   b. that it involves a lack of practicality.
   c. that it is totally inflexible.
   d. that it involves the loss of subjects due to the long period of time required for completion of the research.

4. The theory of development called "nativism" (p. 211):
   a. emphasizes the role of environment.
   b. emphasizes the role of heredity.
   c. easily explains critical periods of development.
   d. holds that experience is the source of all knowledge.

5. The theory of development called "empiricism" (p. 211):
   a. easily explains critical periods of development.
   b. holds that development is nothing more than maturation.
   c. holds that experience is the source of all knowledge.
   d. emphasizes the role of heredity.

6. The notion of "critical periods" suggests that (p. 211):
   a. intelligence is innate.
   b. humans and animals develop differently.
   c. heredity and environment interact to determine development.
   d. cross-cultural studies are preferable in order to determine the effect of heredity on personality.

7. Hubel and Wiesel's research with kittens deprived of visual stimulation (pp. 211-212):
   a. demonstrated the phenomenon of "critical periods."
   b. showed that deprivation damaged cortical cells only if it came between the fourth and twelfth week of life.
   c. showed that kittens must have visual experience during a specific period of life or else their visual system will not develop normally.
   d. all of the above.

8. During the ___________________, the growing organism develops internal organs, limbs with separate fingers and toes, and external sex organs (p. 212).
   a. Period of the Embryo
   b. Period of the Ovum
   c. Period of the Fetus
   d. Period of the Zygote

9. The "age of viability" refers to (p. 214):
   a. conception.
   b. the time at which the fetus might survive if born prematurely.
   c. the age at which the mother can first feel the fetus moving within her.
   d. none of the above.

10. One venereal disease, syphilis, (p. 214):
    a. has no effect on the developing fetus.
    b. can infect the fetus carried by a woman with the disease.
    c. does not infect the fetus if the mother's infection is successfully treated by the fifth month of pregnancy.
    d. b and c above.

11. Which of the following drugs can affect fetal development (p. 214)?
    a. thalidomide
    b. aspirin
    c. nicotine
    d. all of the above.

12. If a pregnant woman has an extremely poor diet, her baby's brain size can be up to ________% smaller at birth (p. 214).
    a. 10
    b. 28
    c. 60
    d. 45

13. Delivery complications (p. 215):
    a. are very frequent, occurring in over 25% of births.
    b. cannot be detected until long after birth.
    c. may involve too much pressure on the brain or too little oxygen being supplied to the brain.
    d. rarely have long-term effects on mental capabilities.

14. The condition of newborns is often assessed using (p. 215):
    a. the Apgar scoring system.
    b. the Davis scoring system.
    c. the Wechsler scale.
    d. none of the above.

15. Which of the following statements concerning infants' bones is *not* true (p. 216)?
    a. Infants' bones are soft at birth.
    b. Infants' bones harden at different rates.
    c. Hand and wrist bones harden early.
    d. Skull bones harden quickly.

16. The nervous system is "unfinished" at birth because (p. 216):
    a. parts of the brain that are present at birth are smaller than they will be in later life.
    b. the newborn's cortex is underdeveloped.
    c. newborns lack myelin sheaths.
    d. all of the above.

17. Which of the following is *not* a reflex present at birth (p. 217)?
    a. the sitting reflex
    b. the dancing reflex
    c. the Moro reflex
    d. the tonic neck reflex

18. Suppose you exposed a newborn to a very loud noise. The infant draws up his or her legs, stretches out the arms, and arches the back. This motor reaction is called (p. 217):
    a. the tonic neck reflex.
    b. the Moro reflex.
    c. the startle reflex.
    d. b and c above.

19. Coughing and sneezing are known as ____________________ reflexes (p. 217).
    a. subsidiary
    b. redundant
    c. protective
    d. secondary

20. When infants are placed on a "visual cliff," (p. 219-220):
    a. they immediately crawl off the cliff.
    b. they fail to perceive the "depth" of the cliff side of the apparatus.
    c. they tend to avoid the deep side, apparently perceiving its depth.
    d. a and b above.

21. If a large ball or a small ball were placed within a young infant's reach, (p. 220):
    a. the infant probably would spread his or her hands out when he or she saw the *large ball*.
    b. the infant would behave exactly the same for the large and small balls.
    c. the infant would not be able to perceive the size difference.
    d. the infant would be "visually confused."

22. Fantz used a "looking box" to determine infants' visual preferences. Which of the following would *not* be a preference of a young infant (p. 221)?
    a. curved lines instead of straight ones
    b. bright colors instead of pastels
    c. things that are stationary instead of things that move
    d. the human face over an equally complex pattern

23. The process of responding in a way that fits existing schema is called (p. 223):
    a. accommodation.
    b. organization.
    c. object permanence.
    d. assimilation.

24. A young infant is looking at a toy. An adult hides the toy from the infant's view. The infant does not search for the toy, acting instead as if it did not exist. The infant lacks (p. 223):
    a. the ability to search for the toy.
    b. object permanence.
    c. the schema for toys.
    d. assimilation.

25. Which of the following sequences of Piagetian stages is in the correct order (pp. 222-226)?
    a. sensorimotor, preoperational, concrete operations, formal operations
    b. preoperational, concrete operations, formal operations, sensorimotor
    c. concrete operations, preoperational, formal operations, sensorimtor
    d. sensorimotor, concrete operations, preoperational, formal operations

26. The tendency to attribute life to inanimate objects is called (p. 225):
    a. egocentrism.
    b. animism.
    c. conservation.
    d. accommodation.

27. During the concrete operational stage of development, children may have trouble (p. 225):
    a. thinking about hypothetical examples.
    b. thinking of all the possible combinations of things.
    c. a and b above.
    d. none of the above.

28. Which of the following is *not* true about language development (pp. 226-227)?
    a. Children produce only sounds from their own language when they babble.
    b. The comprehension of words stays far ahead of the production of words.
    c. Young children use single words to express whole phrases.
    d. Two-word statements are eventually expanded into longer, grammatically correct sentences.

29. Social learning theorists try to explain language development in terms of (p. 227):
    a. reinforcement.
    b. punishment.
    c. rule learning.
    d. imitation.

30. The results of studies attempting to teach primates human language suggest that (pp. 228-229):
    a. chimps and gorillas can learn all aspects of human language.
    b. chimps can clearly learn words.
    c. chimps can clearly learn to generate sentences by combining words in different ways.
    d. b and c above.

31. An infant's smile (p. 230):
    a. is always a social response.
    b. may be influenced by genetic factors since identical twins begin social smiling at about the same time but fraternal twins do not.
    c. is not influenced by environmental conditions.
    d. is only caused by "gas" until 3 months of age.

32. Harlow's experiments with monkeys and substitute mothers demonstrated that (pp. 231-232):
    a. attachments develop only to mothers who provide nourishment.
    b. monkeys will not become attached to substitute (artificial) mothers.
    c. the monkeys preferred and became attached to the terrycloth "mothers."
    d. in stressful situations, the monkeys ignored their terrycloth mothers.

33. Infants who seek their mothers' contact, but then reject and push them away are said to be (p. 227):
    a. securely attached.
    b. unattached.
    c. overattached.
    d. anxiously attached.

34. "Securely attached" infants (p. 228):
    a. are more likely to enjoy problem-solving at 2 or 3 years.
    b. get more involved in problems and work on them longer.
    c. have better relationships with other children.
    d. all of the above.

35. Which of the following has *not* been found to be a characteristic of securely attached babies (p. 232)?
    a. more likely to enjoy problem-solving
    b. more sharing with other children
    c. less fighting with other children
    d. developing language skills earlier

36. The process of copying the behavior of others is called (p. 223):
    a. imitation.
    b. identification.
    c. learning through association.
    d. attachment.

37. Parents teach sex roles to their children by (p. 235):
    a. handling male and female children differently.
    b. modeling sex roles.
    c. having different expectations for boys and girls.
    d. all of the above.

38. When monkeys are raised with their mothers but without other peers (p. 236):
    a. the deprived monkeys sometimes screamed with fear when strange monkeys approached.
    b. the deprived monkeys sometimes were overly aggressive when strange monkeys
       approached.
    c. the deprived monkeys were able to interact appropriately with strange monkeys.
    d. a and b above.

39. First-born children or only children (p. 237):
    a. tend to be more cooperative than later-born children.
    b. tend to be less intelligent than later-born children.
    c. tend to be less cautious than later-born children.
    d. none of the above.

40. Parents treat first-born children differently from later-born children by (p. 237):
    a. spending less time with them.
    b. talking more to them.
    c. exerting less pressure on them.
    d. none of the above.

Answers to Practice Test

1. c	16. d	31. b
2. d	17. a	32. c
3. a	18. d	33. d
4. b	19. c	34. d
5. c	20. c	35. d
6. c	21. a	36. a
7. d	22. c	37. d
8. a	23. d	38. d
9. b	24. b	39. a
10. d	25. b	40. b
11. d	26. b	
12. c	27. c	
13. c	28. a	
14. a	29. d	
15. d	30. b	

1. Suppose you were interested in testing the hypothesis that people born in 1940 are less intelligent than people born in 1960. Suppose, also, that both longitudinal and cross-sectional data are available concerning the IQ's of these two generations. Which type of data would be more appropriate for investigating the problem of interest? Why? Try to think of all the potential problems you would have in interpreting data from a study of intelligence across the generations (for example, differences in quality of education, upbringing, and so forth).

2. One of your good friends has just discovered she is pregnant. What advice would you give her concerning her diet and her exposure to drugs, alcohol, cigarettes, and so forth?

3. Your friend has had her baby. She tells you she's not going to interact much with the infant until he is much older. After all, she says, the baby really does not understand much about the world. What can you tell your friend about the baby's perceptual capabilities that might change her mind?

4. Suppose you are a nursery school teacher. How would you use Piaget's theory of development to design a curriculum for 4- and 5-year olds that would foster their transition into concrete operations?

5. What would language development be like if the child had to rely strictly on imitation, reinforcement, and punishment to guide his or her acquisition of the mother tongue?

Adolescence, Adulthood, and Aging

CHAPTER OUTLINE

Adjusting to the Death of Loved Ones
Accepting Your Own Death

CHAPTER OBJECTIVES

After completing Chapter 8, you should:

1. Be able to explain why Georgia O'Keefe's life challenges traditional developmental approaches, which assume that development moves in a positive direction until maturity, stabilizes, and then declines in late adulthood.

2. Know the difficulties involved in pinpointing exactly when puberty begins, particularly in boys.

3. Realize that moral thought is not always synonymous with moral behavior.

4. Understand why adolescents often have "identity crises," and why these crises may be particularly pronounced in our culture.

5. Be able to explain the relationship between the three methods of parental control and the child's personality.

6. See young adulthood as a time of commitments and potential conflicts among commitments.

7. Be able to compare the development of occupational commitments for career men and career women.

8. Realize that middle adulthood is a traditional phase in the individual's relationship with both children and parents. On the one hand, children are becoming more independent. On the other hand, aging parents are becoming more dependent.

9. Be aware that the "midlife crisis" and "empty-nest syndrome" have been exaggerated by the media and are *not* an unavoidable part of middle-age.

10. Understand that both career "persisters" and career "shifters" can be happy with their lives, depending on their degree of self-direction and on the degree of pressure they feel to switch careers.

11. Know why it is difficult to identify cognitive changes in the elderly.

12. Be able to list ways in which the elderly person's sensory abilities can be maximized through careful design of the environment.

13. Be aware of the different roles grandparents can create when interacting with their grandchildren and why grandparenting has been called the "roleless" role.

14. Be able to explain why marital satisfaction is so high among elderly couples.

15. Be able to identify the factors determining the elderly person's adjustment to retirement.

16. Know the progressive phases an elderly person goes through in adjusting to the death of a loved one or in accepting his or her own impending death.

17. Be aware of the positive and negative sides of adolescence, young adulthood, middle adulthood, and late adulthood, and see that all four periods are times of *development*.

KEY TERMS SELF-TEST

In each group below, fill in the letter of the term on the right with the appropriate definition on the left.

Adolescence

Definitions		**Key Terms**
_B_	1. period extending from age 12 to the late teens	a. puberty (p. 245)
_A_	2. the time in adolescence when sexual reproduction becomes possible	b. adolescence (p. 244)
_D_	3. traits directly concerned with sexual reproduction	c. secondary sexual characteristics (p. 245)
_C_	4. traits typical of a sex, but not directly concerned with reproduction	d. primary sexual characteristics (p. 245)

Adolescence and Young Adulthood

Definitions		**Key Terms**
_C_	1. the beginning of menstruation	a. identity crisis (p. 248)
_D_	2. the process of bringing behavior under the control of inner, personal standards	b. cohabitation (p. 251)
		c. menarche (p. 245)
		d. internalization (p. 246)

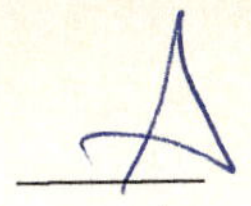

_____ 3. search during adolescence for an
identity which involves testing
different roles

_____ 4. relationship between two unmarried
people who live together

Answers to Key Terms Self-Test

Adolescence	Adolescence and Young Adulthood
1. b	1. c
2. a	2. d
3. d	3. a
4. c	4. b

PRACTICE TEST

Circle the correct letter.

1. The approach that is concerned with the description and explanation of changes in behavior within an individual and differences between individuals from conception to death is called (p. 244):
   a. the traditional developmental approach.
   b. Freud's developmental approach.
   c. the life-span developmental approach.
   d. Piaget's developmental approach.

2. Which of the following is *not* true concerning male and female growth spurts during adolescence (pp. 244-245)?
   a. Most boys are larger than girls between the ages of 11 and 13.
   b. Girls increase their growth rate earlier than boys.
   c. At the age of 10, girls and boys are generally of equal strength.
   d. Boys almost double their strength during their teen years.

3. Benjamin no longer takes cookies from the cookie jar when his mother leaves the house. He has come to realize this is an unacceptable behavior, even when his mother is not there to remind him. According to Kohlberg, Benjamin is beginning to _____________________ his behaviors (p. 246).
   a. rationalize
   b. restrain
   c. internalize
   d. accommodate

4. When children reason that an action is right or wrong because of possible punishment, they are

   at the _______________________ level of moral reasoning in Kohlberg's system (p. 246):
   a. conventional
   b. preconventional
   c. anticonventional
   d. postconventional

5. When children's answers to moral dilemmas are based on abstract principles, they are said to be

   at the _______________________ level of moral reasoning in Kohlberg's system (p. 246):
   a. conventional
   b. preconventional
   c. anticonventional
   d. postconventional

6. Teenagers (p. 247):
   a. are more likely to be at higher levels of moral reasoning than preteens.
   a. cheat *less* than preteens.
   c. cheat when the pressures are great enough.
   d. a and c above.

7. A comparison of Freud's and Erikson's theories shows that (p. 248):
   a. Freud believes that personality is determined by the time we are 6 or 7 years old.
   b. Erikson believes that the issues or events crucial to personality development are always sexual in nature.
   c. Freud believes that personality continues to grow and change throughout our lifetime.
   d. neither Freud nor Erikson believes that people go through stages of personality development.

8. In comparing early- and late-maturing children, researchers have found that (p. 249):
   a. boys who mature late often feel inadequate.
   b. late-maturing girls tend to be less self-confident and relaxed in social relationships.
   c. early-maturing boys tend to be leaders, especially in sports.
   d. all of the above.

9. When parents provide little or no control of their children's behavior and are relatively uninterested in their children's input into decision-making, they can be said to be

   _______________________ (pp. 249-250):
   a. authoritarian.
   b. authoritative.
   c. permissive.
   d. relaxed.

10. Dunphy observed that peer-group structures of urban teenagers progress through five stages. Which of the following orderings of the final three stages is correct (p. 251)?
   a. crowds, dating, fully mixed boy-girl cliques
   b. dating, crowds, fully mixed boy-girl cliques
   c. crowds, fully mixed boy-girl cliques, dating
   d. dating, fully mixed boy-girl cliques, crowds

11. Which of the following is *not* true about pregnant teenagers (p. 251)?
   a. The United States has one of the lowest teenage pregnancy rates in the world.
   b. Two-thirds of teenage pregnancies are accidental.
   c. Teenage pregnancies increase the risk of physical complications for both mother and child.
   d. Pregnant teenagers who do get married often get divorced later on.

12. Lowenthal argues that young adults make three particularly important commitments. Which of the following is *not* on Lowenthal's list (p. 252)?
   a. life style
   b. moral
   c. interpersonal
   d. mastery

13. One of the major findings of the research conducted on events composing a family cycle is that (p. 253):
   a. the average ages of women during these events were almost exactly the same for the different social classes.
   b. upper-middle class women were usually 1 to 2 years younger than lower-class women for each event.
   c. the time span between first and last child is very different between socio-economic groups.
   d. most women, regardless of these social classes, get married 3 to 5 years after leaving their parents' homes.

14. Which of the following aspects of personality and social development is (are) associated with careers, according to White (p. 254)?
   a. respond to people warmly and respectfully
   b. base decisions upon own beliefs
   c. respect cultural values
   d. all of the above

15. When researchers have compared homemakers and working women, they have found that (pp. 255-256):
   a. working women are generally more satisfied with life than homemakers.
   b. the main source of satisfaction and esteem for the working woman is her career.
   c. working women feel they pay less attention to their husbands than homemakers.
   d. the main source of satisfaction and esteem for the homemaker is her children's approval.

16. Successful career women (p. 256):
    a. have fathers who were extremely supportive of their careers.
    b. tended to be later-born children.
    c. tended to be average college students.
    d. rejected assistance from senior male executives from the beginning of their careers onward.

17. Between the early thirties and age 40, men go through a period in which they emphasize stability and security. This period is called by Levison (p. 257):
    a. midlife crisis.
    b. settling down.
    c. the transitional period.
    d. none of the above.

18. According to Erikson, a sense of producing and contributing to the world is called:
    a. stagnation.
    b. generativity.
    c. productivity.
    d. satisfaction drive.

19. The "empty-nest syndrome" (p. 268):
    a. refers to the negative feelings connected with children leaving home.
    b. has probably been exaggerated by the media.
    c. is called into question by the high levels of life satisfaction parents often report after their youngest child leaves home.
    d. all of the above.

20. The "midlife crisis" (pp. 268-269):
    a. is an unavoidable consequence of middle adulthood.
    b. may be exception rather than the rule.
    c. tends to occur in middle-aged people who were also not well adjusted as adolescents or young adults.
    d. b and c above.

21. Which of the following is a physical change that occurs during middle adulthood (pp. 259-260)?
    a. substantial weight loss
    b. myelinization of brain cells
    c. reduced lung capacity
    d. reduced bladder capacity

22. Biological changes in middle adulthood (p. 269):
    a. have a dramatic effect on the everyday lives of most middle-agers.
    b. have little effect on the everyday lives of most middle-agers.
    c. cause considerable concern, particularly among middle-aged men.
    d. b and c above.

23. According to your authors, the key to parent-child harmony in middle-adulthood is (p. 261):
   a. giving adolescent children total freedom.
   b. carefully restricting the freedom of adolescent children.
   c. mutual respect for the rights of both children and parents.
   d. none of the above.

24. Midlife career shifts for men (p. 262):
   a. are often satisfying, productive, and orderly.
   b. are more likely to be positive in blue-collar workers than in white-collar workers.
   c. are *not* influenced by personality or situational factors.
   d. none of the above.

25. One type of career "persister" among females involves (p. 262):
   a. women who stay with the same company through young adulthood and middle adulthood.
   b. women who remain full-time homemakers.
   c. women who interrupt their outside-the-home careers to raise children.
   d. a and b above.

26. According to one theory of aging, cell malfunctions in elderly people (p. 263):
   a. are caused in part by mutations that damage genes.
   b. interfere with the normal operation of physiological systems.
   c. lead to physical changes we know as aging.
   d. all of the above.

27. Jerome's experiment on problem-solving abilities (pp. 264-265):
   a. demonstrated that aging causes a clear decline in problem-solving ability.
   b. is difficult to interpret because the two age-groups may have differed in their motivation to solve the assigned problems.
   c. is difficult to interpret because the two age-groups may have differed in educational experience.
   d. b and c above.

28. Which of the following is *not* a cognitive change that Botwinick states occurs with age (p. 265)?
   a. Older people need more time to respond in learning situations.
   b. Elderly people tend to be more insecure.
   c. Elderly people's short-term memory is better for things they see than for things they hear.
   d. Elderly people tend to resist learning things that seem to them to be irrelevant and meaningless.

29. To maximize the elderly person's ability to hear you, you should (p. 264):
   a. speak in low-pitched sounds.
   b. speak in high-pitched sounds.
   c. shout to be heard.
   d. none of the above.

30. Vision is impaired in the elderly in which of the following ways (p. 264)?
    a. There is a reduction in the ability to see depth.
    b. Objects located in the center of the person's vision are most difficult to see.
    c. Blues, greens, and violets are difficult to see.
    d. a and c above.

31. The most common styles of grandparenting are (p. 266):
    a. surrogate-parent and distant figure.
    b. fun-seeking and formal.
    c. fun-seeking and distant figure.
    d. reservoir of family wisdom and formal.

32. When a grandparent adopts the "reservoir of family wisdom" style of grandparenting, he or she (p. 266):
    a. engages in mutually satisfying leisure activities with the grandchildren.
    b. interacts very little with the grandchildren.
    c. gives instruction for special skills and is authoritarian.
    d. assumes care-giving responsibilities.

33. Marital satisfaction (p. 267):
    a. is very high for elderly couples.
    b. tends to decline in late adulthood because couples stop expressing feelings.
    c. is made difficult by the great deal of time elderly couples spend together.
    d. tends to decline in late adulthood because couples stop enjoying sexual contact.

34. When the attitudes of men and women toward retirement are compared (p. 270):
    a. men with high socioeconomic status and leisure-time interests tend to plan for their retirement.
    b. men with high socioeconomic status and leisure-time interests have a negative attitude toward retirement.
    c. women with high-status jobs and high income are anxious to retire.
    d. none of the above.

35. Career women are often better prepared to adjust to retirement than career men because (p. 270):
    a. they have a more positive attitude toward retirement.
    b. the role of homemaker is a traditionally acceptable substitute activity for time previously spent on the job.
    c. they are more likely to find another job after retirement.
    d. they did not really want to work anyway.

36. Comparison of the attitudes of retirees before and after retirement indicate that (p. 270):
    a. 33 percent found retirement to be better than they had anticipated.
    b. 5 percent found retirement to be worse than they anticipated.
    c. most people adjusted well to retirement and were satisfied with life.
    d. all of the above.

37. According to Erikson, the last stage of development involves the crisis of (p. 270):
    a. identity vs. isolation.
    b. generativity vs. stagnation.
    c. trust vs. mistrust.
    d. integrity vs. despair.

38. The "initial response" to the death of a spouse is a phase characterized by (p. 271):
    a. worry of a nervous breakdown.
    b. an obsessional review of how the death could have been prevented.
    c. shock and overwhelming sorrow.
    d. disbelief and denial.

39. The correct sequence of the first three stages in Kubler-Ross's description of adjustment to death is (pp. 271-272):
    a. anger, denial and isolation, bargaining.
    b. denial and isolation, bargaining, anger.
    c. denial and isolation, anger, bargaining.
    d. bargaining, denial and isolation, anger.

40. Reactive depression refers to (p. 272):
    a. a sense of impending loss of everything and everyone you love.
    b. feeling downcast because of people and things that need to be taken care of.
    c. a and b.
    d. none of the above.

Answers to Practice Test

1. c	11. a	21. c	31. b
2. a	12. a	22. d	32. c
3. c	13. c	23. c	33. a
4. b	14. d	24. a	34. a
5. d	15. b	25. d	35. b
6. d	16. a	26. d	36. d
7. a	17. b	27. d	37. d
8. d	18. b	28. c	38. c
9. c	19. d	29. a	39. c
10. b	20. d	30. d	40. b

1. Traditionally, adolescence has been seen as a time of tremendous change, a stormy time of emotional upheaval. Compared to the other periods of development covered in Chapter 8, are the adjustments and life changes in adolescence really that much more dramatic?

2. Many of you were raised in fairly traditional homes in which the mother was a homemaker and the father a "breadwinner." What problems might a female raised in such an environment have in making family and occupational commitments in young adulthood?

3. In describing middle adulthood, your authors suggested that the "midlife crisis" and the "empty nest syndrome" might be myths rather than unavoidable consequences of middle-age. What other "myths" do we have concerning other periods of adolescence and adult development? How might these myths interfere with our ability to understand development across the life-span?

4. Suppose you are having a discussion with your middle-aged parent. Your parent is depressed thinking about getting older. What can you tell him or her about the *positive* side of aging?

9

Motivation

CHAPTER OBJECTIVES

After completing Chapter 9, you should:

1. Know what is meant by the term "motive," and know the difference between primary and social motives.

2. Understand three different theories of motivation.

3. Know what a hierarchy of motives is, and know the probable order of some motives in a hierarchy.

4. Know some of the factors which influence when, how much, and what we eat.

5. Understand some of the differences between obese and normal people in their eating patterns.

6. Be able to describe some of the biological determinants of sexual behavior.

7. Know the roles of external cues and learning in the release of sexual behavior in humans.

8. Know the approximate rates of masturbation, premarital sex, marital sex, and homosexuality in our society.

9. Understand that people have a motivation to seek stimulation and how this motive is hard to explain with some theories of motivation.

10. Be able to describe how one might observe people satisfying their motive to affiliate and know what factors influence their desire to affiliate.

11. Understand that there are several theories to explain our motivation to aggress and that these theories lead to different conclusions concerning the role of aggression in preventing/promoting future aggression.

12. Know how the viewing of aggression may influence the tendency to act aggressively.

13. Know how achievement motivation is defined and what developmental factors may affect achievement motivation.

14. Be able to describe some of the desirable and undesirable characteristics of people with high achievement motivation.

In each group below, fill in the letter of the term on the right with the appropriate definition on the left.

The Nature of Motivation

Definitions

1. motives such as hunger, thirst, and the need for air and rest
2. motives that come from learning and social interaction
3. innate predispositions to act in specific ways
4. a tension or state that results when a need is not met
5. the attempt by the body to maintain a constant internal state
6. cells in the hypothalamus that monitor the glucose content of the blood
7. units of energy used when food is used by the body

Key Terms

a. glucoreceptors (p. 282)
b. primary motives (p. 276)
c. homeostasis (p. 278)
d. instincts (p. 277)
e. drive (p. 278)
f. calories (p. 283)
g. social motives (p. 277)

Sexual Motivation

Definitions

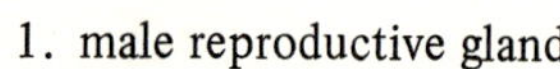
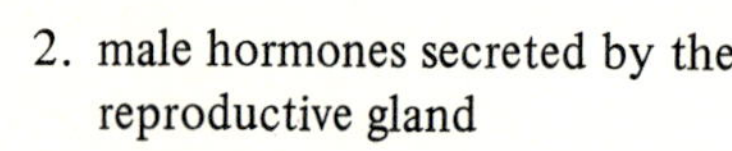

1. male reproductive gland
2. male hormones secreted by the reproductive gland
3. female reproductive glands
4. female sex hormone
5. in women, the time when the egg is available to be fertilized
6. self-manipulation of one's genitals
7. sexual desire for those of the same sex as oneself

Key Terms

a. masturbation (p. 288)
b. estrogen (p. 287)
c. ovaries (p. 287)
d. testes (p. 286)
e. androgens (p. 286)
f. homosexuality (p. 290)
g. ovulation (p. 287)

Other Major Motives

Definitions   **Key Terms**

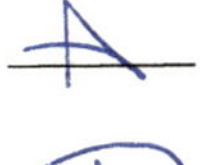

_____ 1. motive to explore and manipulate   a. aggression cues (p. 296)
         new objects   b. stimulus-seeking motive (p. 291)
                                                    c. frustration (p. 295)
_____ 2. motive to associate with other people   d. achievement motive (p. 299)
                                                    e. displaced aggression (p. 295)
_____ 3. the result of being blocked from   f. affiliation motive (p. 292)
         getting what you want

_____ 4. taking out one's anger and/or
         frustration on someone or
         something other than the cause
         of one's anger

_____ 5. stimuli that a person has learned to
         associate with aggression

_____ 6. motive to do things as rapidly and/or
         as well as possible

Answers to Key Term Self-Test

The Nature of Motivation   **Other Major Motives**
1. b   5. c   1. b   4. e
2. g   6. a   2. f   5. a
3. d   7. f   3. c   6. d
4. e

Sexual Motivation
1. d   5. g
2. e   6. a
3. c   7. f
4. b

PRACTICE TEST

Circle the correct letter.

1. Motives which concern our biological needs are called (p. 276):
    a. secondary motives.
    b. primary motives.
    c. social motives
    d. biological motives.

2. Motives such as affiliation, aggression, and achievement are probably (p. 277):
   a. secondary motives.
   b. primary motives.
   c. social motives.
   d. biological motives.

3. One theory of motivation has at its core the idea that inborn predispositions control our behavior. This theory is called (p. 277):
   a. instinct theory.
   b. Freud's theory.
   c. drive theory.
   d. incentive theory.

4. The theory of motivation based on inborn predispositions has declined in favor because (p. 277):
   a. drives are difficult to define.
   b. man is seldom impelled to action.
   c. of the great variety found in human behavior.
   d. of the thumb-twiddling instinct.

5. The basis of the drive theory of motivation is (p. 279):
   a. tension.
   b. instinct.
   c. the effects of learning on behavior.
   d. homeostasis.

6. An example of a primary motive is
   a. greed.
   b. thirst.
   c. wantonness.
   d. piety.

7. Five-year-old Daniel spied a clock on the shelf. Using a screw driver, he completely disassembled the timepiece. What theory of motivation would explain his behavior?
   a. social learning
   b. incentive theory
   c. drive-reduction theory
   d. instinct theory

8. The thermostat in a house is a good example of the mechanism involved in which of the theories of motivation (p. 278)?
   a. incentive theory
   b. drive theory
   c. instinct theory
   d. all of the above

9. Humans engage in many activities for the purpose of increasing arousal. This fact is used in support of which of the theories of motivation (p. 279)?
   a. incentive theory
   b. drive theory
   c. instinct theory
   d. hierarchy theory

10. We can view _________________ theories as "push" theories, while _____________________ theories of motivation are "pull" theories (p. 279).
   a. drive/instinct
   b. drive/incentive
   c. incentive/drive
   d. incentive/instinct

11. Which of the following people is associated with the idea of a hierarchy of motives (pp. 279-280)?
   a. Sir Edmund Hillary
   b. Holt
   c. Hull
   d. Maslow

12. According to the hierarchy of needs, which of the following needs must be satisfied before the other needs can influence behavior (p. 280)?
   a. order and safety
   b. affiliation
   c. hunger
   d. achievement

13. Maslow's theory of motivation has been criticised because (p. 280):
   a. it is a drive-reduction theory.
   b. of the specific ordering of some of his motives.
   c. hunger is a drive-reducing motive.
   d. all of the above.

14. Studies investigating the relation between hunger and physiological activities have found (p. 281):
   a. feelings of hunger often occur at the same time as stomach contractions.
   b. stomach contractions are controlled when we start to eat.
   c. a full stomach often leads a person to stop eating.
   d. a and c above.

15. When the nerves to an animal's stomach are cut so that the animal's brain does not "know" of stomach contractions (p. 281):
   a. the animal will eat continuously.
   b. the animal will refuse food.
   c. the animal will continue to eat normally.
   d. the animal will die.

16. Studies have found that humans injected with insulin reported feeling hungry. This demonstrates that (p. 282):
   a. the hypothalamus contains glucoreceptors.
   b. the level of glucose in the blood affects our feeling of hunger.
   c. insulin is used to treat diabetes.
   d. all of the above.

17. When certain areas of the hypothalamus are stimulated with electrical current (p. 282):
   a. animals will start to eat.
   b. animals will stop eating, even when hungry.
   c. animals will start to eat, *but* only when they are hungry.
   d. a and b above.

18. In addition to the hypothalamus, what other place in the body monitors blood-sugar level (p. 292)?
   a. the liver
   b. the stomach
   c. the temporal lobe
   d. the pancreas

19. Experiments on the role of the hypothalamus in eating have shown that (p. 282):
   a. destruction of certain areas has no effect on eating behavior while stimulation will result in a change in eating behavior.
   b. destruction of certain areas affects eating while stimulation has no effect.
   c. both destruction and stimulation of certain areas will increase eating but will have no effect on decreasing eating.
   d. both destruction and stimulation of certain areas will affect both increasing and decreasing eating behavior.

20. The digestion of foods, especially those high in protein, causes body temperature to (p. 283):
   a. rise.
   b. fall.
   c. fluctuate.
   d. remain stable.

110

21. Which of the following is probably responsible for the long-term maintenance of body weight
(p. 283)?
   a. sensory receptors sensitive to body weight
   b. metabolism
   c. cells in the hypothalamus that keep track of fat deposits
   d. level of activity

22. Compared to short-term mechanisms of eating behavior, long-term mechanisms of body weight
(p. 283):
   a. are controlled by the hypothalamus.
   b. are controlled by a different system.
   c. are controlled by learned habits.
   d. are sensitive to calories eaten.

23. When infants are allowed to choose their diet over a period of months (p. 283):
   a. on any given day the infants might choose a "bad diet."
   b. each day the infants choose a balanced diet.
   c. over a long period of time the infants developed dietary deficiencies.
   d. a and c above.

24. Rats may continue to choose a sugar diet over a salt diet, even when they need the salt to
survive. This is an example of (p. 284):
   a. the role of the adrenal gland in controlling diet.
   b. the selection of foods to meet dietary requirements.
   c. the role of learning in food selection.
   d. none of the above.

25. Obese people are more likely than normal-weight people to (p. 284):
   a. eat by the clock.
   b. eat when they have to work to get food.
   c. be sensitive to internal cues.
   d. all of the above.

26. Which of the following is not an external cue which affects eating behavior in obese people
(pp. 284-285)?
   a. time
   b. taste of the food
   c. arousal
   d. appearance of the food

27. When obese and normal weight people watch an exciting movie or a travelogue (p. 285):
   a. obese subjects eat a lot more after seeing the arousing films than after the travelogue.
   b. obese subjects eat more after seeing the travelogue than after the arousing films.
   c. normal-weight individuals eat more after the arousing films than after the travelogue.
   d. a and c above.

28. Which of the following would be considered an important factor associated with obesity?
    a. interpreting external cues
    b. becoming sensitive to internal cues
    c. physical disorders
    d. interpreting internal cues

29. In humans androgens influence the development of (p. 286):
    a. primary sex characteristics.
    b. secondary sex characteristics.
    c. the ovaries.
    d. sex drive in females.

30. Sexual behavior in male dogs (p. 286):
    a. continues normally if the animals are castrated after they have reached maturity.
    b. has definite biological cycles.
    c. can be elicited only from animals with intact sexual organs.
    d. can be elicited even if castration is performed before the animal reached sexual maturity.

31. The secretion of estrogen is at its highest level during (p. 287):
    a. copulation.
    b. ovulation.
    c. puberty.
    d. masturbation.

32. Which of the following is *not* a determinant of the human female's sex drive (p. 287):
    a. objects associated with sex
    b. interaction with peers during childhood
    c. level of estrogen
    d. learning

33. Humans can be sexually aroused by an almost inconceivable range of stimuli. This observation demonstrates (p. 287):
    a. the role of hormones in controlling sexual behavior.
    b. that humans are capricious lovers.
    c. that human males have a normally high level of androgen.
    d. the role of learning in human sexual behavior.

34. Human sexual responses can be categorized into four phases. These phases, in the order of their occurrence, are (p. 288):
    a. excitement phase, plateau phase, orgasm phase, resolution period.
    b. plateau phase, excitement phase, resolution period, orgasm phase.
    c. arousal phase, refractory phase, orgasm phase, resolution period.
    d. arousal phase, erection phase, orgasm phase, resolution period.

35. Which of the following phases of sexual responses is characteristic of human males but not human females (p. 288)?
    a. orgasm phase
    b. refractory phase
    c. arousal phase
    d. resolution period

36. A recent survey of sexual behavior has found that among married men over the age of 30, _________________ engage in masturbation.
    a. 90 percent
    b. over half
    c. very few
    d. 45 percent

37. Positive attitudes toward masturbation are associated with (p. 289):
    a. easier arousal in women by sexually explicit pictures.
    b. emotional trauma.
    c. premarital sex.
    d. none of the above.

38. The number of people who engage exclusively in homosexual behavior (p. 291):
    a. as high as 45 percent.
    b. about 4 percent.
    c. between 60 and 80 percent.
    d. 30 percent.

39. When infant monkeys are raised in social isolation and then placed in a cage with other monkeys when they are 1 year old (p. 293):
    a. their desire to affiliate increases.
    b. they avoid social contact.
    c. they take the opportunity to play with peers.
    d. they have a natural drive to affiliate.

40. The relationship between fear and affiliation, according to Schachter, (p. 294):
    a. is inversely proportioned.
    b. appears stronger in later-born children.
    c. appears stronger in first-born children.
    d. is a myth.

41. According to the frustration-aggression theory (p. 295):
    a. frustration always leads to aggression.
    b. aggression is always a consequence of frustration.
    c. aggression always leads to frustration.
    d. a and b above.

42. According to social-learning theory of aggression (p. 296):
   a. aggression occurs as a result of learning.
   b. mechanisms for the learning of aggression are reinforcement and imitation.
   c. watching violent television increases the tendency of viewers to act violently.
   d. all of the above.

Answers to Practice Test

1. b	22. b
2. a	23. a
3. a	24. c
4. c	25. a
5. d	26. c
6. b	27. a
7. b	28. d
8. b	29. b
9. a	30. a
10. b	31. b
11. d	32. c
12. c	33. d
13. b	34. a
14. d	35. b
15. c	36. b
16. b	37. a
17. d	38. b
18. a	39. b
19. d	40. c
20. a	41. d
21. c	42. d

THOUGHT QUESTIONS/APPLICATIONS

1. Many athletes endure great physical discomfort in the preparation for and during competition. What theory of motivation can best explain the behavior of such athletes? How does this theory explain their behavior?

2. Certain levels of body fat are often associated with particular cultures. For example, Italian women are often heavier than oriental women. To what can we attribute these cultural differences in body weight? Consider several different potential sources of these differences.

3. Based on differences between normal and obese eating patterns, how might one change one's life style so it would be less conducive to overeating?

4. Take the role of a staunch conservative clergyman. How might you react to the statistics summarizing sexual behavior in humans? Now defend the position of psychologists who think that the publication of such statistics might have positive social consequences.

10

Emotions and Stress

CHAPTER OUTLINE

CHAPTER OBJECTIVES

After completing Chapter 10, you should:

1. Understand the difference between emotions and motivation.

2. Know that there are a number of different theories of emotions and that each theory of emotion assigns a different role to physiological responses.

3. Understand the nature of nonverbal communication of emotions through facial expressions and body language.

4. Know that the expression of some emotions seems to be innate and invariant across cultures.

5. Be able to describe how lie detection is based on the relation between emotions and physiological activities.

6. Understand the concept of anxiety, its functions in protecting us, and the consequences of different levels of anxiety.

7. Understand that the emotional response of love can be broken down into several components and that a distinction is often made between romantic love and mature love.

8. Know what the effects of learning and arousal are on love.

9. Understand the relation between stress and the general adaptation syndrome.

10. Be able to list some of the major causes of stress.

11. Understand how psychophysiological disorders are caused by excessive stress.

12. Be able to describe some of the consequences of the stress of captivity, such as delayed stress reaction, and the Stockholm Syndrome..

13. Know the differences between Type A and Type B behavior patterns and how they are related to psychophysiological disorders.

14. Know the variety of mechanisms people use to cope with stress.

In each group below, fill in the letter of the term on the right with the appropriate definition on the left.

The Nature of Emotions and Stress

Definitions

1. affective states or feelings accompanied by physiological changes

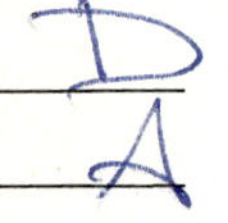

2. the study of body language

3. reaction to a specific danger in the environment

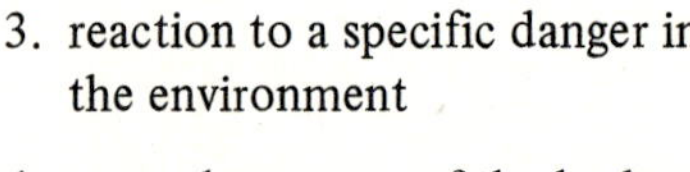

4. general response of the body to any demand made on it

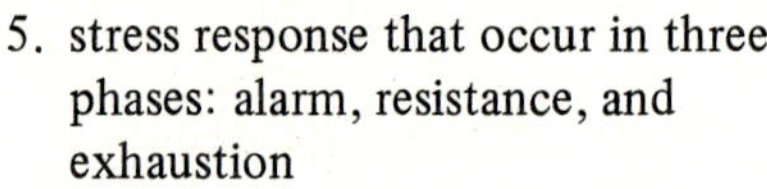

5. stress response that occur in three phases: alarm, resistance, and exhaustion

6. physical illness in which stress is a contributing factor

7. coronary-prone behavior pattern

8. the feeling that one's actions do not affect one's environment

Key Terms

a. fear (p. 321)
b. learned helplessness (p. 336)
c. general adaptation syndrome (p. 325)
d. kinesis (p. 320)
e. emotions (p. 308)
f. stress (p. 325)
g. Type A behavior (p. 335)
h. psychophysiological disorders (p. 332)

Defense Mechanisms

Definitions

1. ways of coping with anxiety

2. the blocking of unpleasant thoughts or memories from conscious awareness

3. consciously blocking or avoiding unpleasant thoughts

4. redirecting an emotion from the person who caused it to another

Key Terms

a. repression (p. 338)
b. sublimation (p. 338)
c. reaction formation (p. 339)
d. suppression (p. 338)
e. defense mechanisms (p. 337)
f. projection (p. 339)
g. displacement (p. 338)

5. rechanneling the energy associated
   with one emotion or event into a
   seemingly unrelated activity

6. seeing our own shortcomings or
   undesirable traits in other people
   rather than in ourselves

7. concealing unacceptable impulses by
   expressing the opposite impulse

Answers to Key Terms Self-Test

The Nature of Emotions and Stress

1. e	5. c
2. d	6. h
3. a	7. g
4. f	8. b

Defense Mechanisms

1. e	5. b
2. a	6. f
3. d	7. c
4. g	

PRACTICE TEST

Circle the correct letter.

1. Emotions, unlike motives, are (p. 308):
   a. difficult to define.
   b. something that we feel.
   c. directly observable.
   d. related to drive states.

2. The physiological effects associated with most emotions are influenced by the (p. 308):
   a. sympathetic nervous system.
   b. parasympathetic nervous system.
   c. hypothalamus.
   d. endocrine system.

3. The parasympathetic nervous system is concerned with (p. 308):
   a. prepring the body for action.
   b. stimulating the adrenal glands.
   c. returning the body to a normal resting state.
   d. all of the above.

4. According to the James-Lange theory of emotions (p. 309):
   a. emotions cause changes in body functions.
   b. physiological changes precede the feeling of emotion.
   c. bodily changes and the feeling of an emotion occur at the same time.
   d. emotions are the result of the perception of physiological changes.

5. Which of the following is not a physiological change associated with emotion (pp. 308-309)?
   a. adrenalin secretion
   b. saliva secretion
   c. increased perspiration
   d. increased breathing

6. Which of the following is not a physiological response measured by the polygraph in the detection of lies (p. 310)?
   a. heart rate
   b. secretion of saliva
   c. blood pressure
   d. galvanic skin response

7. The operator of the polygraph usually asks a series of baseline questions against which to judge responses to critical questions. Which of the following would not be a good baseline question (p. 310)?
   a. How old are you?
   b. What is your name?
   c. Where was the object before it was stolen?
   d. Do you feel nervous?

8. One theory of emotion is that events activate the thalamus, which sends messages to the cerebral cortex leading to the emotional experience. This theory is called (p. 312):
   a. Cannon-Bard Theory.
   b. Two-Factor Theory.
   c. Schachter and Singer Theory
   d. James-Lange Theory.

9. According to the Schachter and Singer cognitive theory of emotions, the physiological arousal accompanying emotion is (p. 312):
   a. unique to each emotion.
   b. reduced if the sympathetic nervous system is removed.
   c. very diffuse and the same arousal patterns can be found in different emotions.
   d. confined to the thalamus.

10. The interpretation of physiological arousal is the basis of the ______________________ theory of emotion (pp. 312-313):
    a. Valins
    b. Cannon-Bard
    c. Schachter and Singer
    d. James-Lange

11. Mamie was afraid to go to school. Ada had told her that the teachers were mean and made children stand in the closet. Mamie's hear pounded as she sucked her thumb while she rode the bus to school. Her behavioral response to fear was (pp. 311-313):
    a. being afraid.
    b. sucking her thumb.
    c. riding the bus.
    d. her heart's pounding.

12. Schachter and Singer found that when subjects were injected with epinephrine they (p. 313):
    a. labeled their arousal as anger.
    b. labeled their emotion as happiness.
    c. labeled unexplained arousal based on the actions of the confederate.
    d. labeled explained arousal based on the actions of the confederate.

13. In one experiment on the effects of perceived arousal on emotions, subjects looked at pictures of nudes and listened to what they believed was their heart rate. The results of this study indicated that (p. 314):
    a. subjects used perceived, not actual, arousal as the basis for labeling their likes and dislikes.
    b. subjects used their actual level of arousal as the basis for labeling their likes and dislikes.
    c. heart rate was a poor indicator of physical attraction.
    d. changes in skin temperature were related to perceived changes in heart rate.

14. One line of research indicates that expectancy may influence the perception of an emotion. This suggests that (pp. 314-315):
    a. after a number of people have told you that you look tired, you may begin to "feel" tired.
    b. when you "feel" tired you may expect people to say you look tired.
    c. how you feel and how you expect to feel are unrelated.
    d. feeling tired makes you look tired.

15. It has been suggested that the first step in experiencing emotions is appraising the situation. This means that (p. 315):
    a. our emotions determine how we interpret the situation.
    b. how we interpret a situation influences our emotions.
    c. judgement of an event occurs as the result of an emotional reaction.
    d. an emotional reaction comes first, then we appraise the situaion.

16. Investigators _____________________ about the components of emotion, but they

    _____________________ about how these components combine to yield a specific feeling (pp. 315-316):
    a. disagree/agree
    b. agree/disagree
    c. know/speculate
    d. speculate/know

17. Darwin needed to show two things to support his evolutionary theory of emotions. One of these things was (p. 317):
    a. that monkeys show emotions.
    b. emotions are expressed the same way by all people regardless of background.
    c. people learn to express emotions in particular ways.
    d. different people express emotions according to their backgrounds.

18. Cross-cultural studies on the expression of emotion (p. 318):
    a. demonstrate some degree of universality in emotional expression.
    b. prove that the expression of emotion is innate.
    c. demonstrate that various societies learn to express emotion in similar ways.
    d. all of the above.

19. The results of one study on the expression of emotion indicated that (p. 318):
    a. the eyes are most important in communicating emotion.
    b. the mouth played a large role in the communication of surprise.
    c. the forehead is important in the communication of happiness.
    d. all three parts of the face are necessary to clearly communicate some emotions.

20. Zelma's jaw is clenched, her brow furrowed, her eyes narrowed, and her face scarlet. She is most likely feeling (p. 319):
    a. contempt.
    b. fear.
    c. anger.
    d. disgust.

21. The study of body language is called (p. 320):
    a. body linguistics.
    b. kinesis.
    c. kinesthetics.
    d. kinesiology.

22. In terms of body language, people telling a lie (p. 320):
    a. show less body movement.
    b. smile.
    c. keep a greater distance from the listener.
    d. all of the above.

23. As compared to objective anxiety, neurotic anxiety is the result of (p. 321):
    a. apprehension.
    b. a specific danger in the environment.
    c. unconscious conflict within the person.
    d. fear of the unknown.

24. Fear has important functions in our lives. Which of the following is not a positive function of fear (p. 322)?
    a. It leads us to avoid dangerous objects and situations.
    b. It may lead to "tunnel vision."
    c. It prepares the body for action.
    d. It often leads to the strengthening of social bonds.

25. According to the Yerkes-Dodson principle, the relation between arousal and performance is (p. 322):
    a. high levels of arousal aid work.
    b. low levels of arousal aid work.
    c. high levels of arousal will aid work on a difficult task.
    d. high levels of arousal are disruptive of performance on difficult tasks.

26. Love has been defined as an emotion involving three components: Which of the following is *not* one of these components (p. 323)?
    a. caring
    b. communication
    c. attachment
    d. intimacy

27. Monkeys removed from their mothers during infancy and raised in isolation exhibited strong effects of their past experience. These effects included (p. 324):
    a. the inability to play with age-mates.
    b. unreceptiveness to sexual advances from other monkeys.
    c. failure to feed and care for their offspring.
    d. all of the above.

28. In some social circles, parachuting is considered an aphrodisiac. This effect of parachuting on sexual excitement might be interpreted as an effect of _________________ on love (p. 324):
    a. learning
    b. falling
    c. arousal
    d. context

29. Stress is (p. 325):
    a. an emotion.
    b. a general response of the body.
    c. a state of mind.
    d. a and b above.

30. The general adaptation syndrome has three phases. These phases, in order, are (p. 325):
    a. alarm reaction, stage of resistance, stage of exhaustion.
    b. fear reaction, stage of alarm, stage of resistance.
    c. alarm reaction, stage of exhaustion, stage of resistance.
    d. fear reaction, stage of exhaustion, death.

31. The Holmes Life Change Scale assigns stress values to life events. The reasoning behind this
    scale is (p. 327):
    a. that change in a person's life leads to stress, which in turn leads to illness.
    b. that illness leads to a change in a person's life which produces additional stress.
    c. that common hassles are irritating and frustrating and thus produce stress.
    d. based on the assumption that only negative changes are stress producing.

32. In the comparison of the medical records of air-traffic controllers with other airmen, the
    controllers were significantly more likely to suffer from a variety of illnesses. This demonstrates
    the effects of (p. 329):
    a. age on illness.
    b. unpredictability on stress.
    c. pressure on health.
    d. arousal on health.

33. Having the chance to control one's life (pp. 330-331):
    a. is stress producing, even though it is a positive experience.
    b. tends to be stress producing, since one has added responsibility.
    c. tends to be stress reducing.
    d. has no effect on stress.

34. Conflict occurs almost every time you make a choice; the degree of conflict is determined by
    (p. 331):
    a. your overall level of stress.
    b. how equally the choices are matched in attractiveness.
    c. whether or not the conflict is an approach-approach conflict or an avoidance-avoidance
        conflict.
    d. how close we are to the goal.

35. Kelly's first job offer in the circus involved being a clown. This created conflict because on the
    one hand he would be earning money, while on the other hand he knew nothing about
    clowning. This is an example of (pp. 331-332):
    a. an approach-approach conflict.
    b. an avoidance-avoidance conflict.
    c. approach-avoidance conflict.
    d. a double approach-avoidance conflict.

36. Psychophysiological disorders, often called psychosomatic illnesses, are (p. 332):
    a. real physical illnesses in which stress is a contributing factor.
    b. a result of stress whereby one thinks one is ill but does not have a real physical illness.
    c. physical illnesses accompanied by psychological stress.
    d. the result of a stress-producing physical illness.

37. Symptoms of the delayed stress reaction include (p. 334):
   a. depression and anxiety.
   b. the inability to concentrate.
   c. insomnia.
   d. all of the above.

38. The coronary-prone behavior pattern is also called (p. 335):
   a. Type A behavior.
   b. Type B behavior.
   c. psychosomatic illness.
   d. running on nervous energy.

39. Seligman demonstrated that if dogs experience inescapable shocks, they later fail to learn to avoid an escapable shock. This is called (p. 336):
   a. experimental neurosis.
   b. regression.
   c. learned helplessness.
   d. avoidance learning.

40. Which of the following defense mechanisms involves a conscious effort to block or avoid thinking about an event (p. 338)?
   a. repression
   b. suppression
   c. displacement
   d. sublimation

Answers to Practice Test

1. b	11. b	21. b	31. a
2. a	12. c	22. d	32. b
3. c	13. a	23. c	33. c
4. d	14. a	24. b	34. b
5. b	15. b	25. d	35. b
6. b	16. b	26. b	36. a
7. c	17. b	27. d	37. d
8. a	18. a	28. c	38. a
9. c	19. d	29. b	39. c
10. c	20. c	30. a	40. b

1. Consider the various theories of emotions. What do these theories have in common? How do these theories compare to your own views on the psychology of emotions?

2. Consider the idea that the expression of some emotions is innate. For example, smiling may be a "prewired" means to express pleasure. What role might this have in parent-infant interactions? Can you see how this may be beneficial to the preservation of the species?

3. In the text it is argued that major life changes cause stress, which in turn lead to physical illness. Reanalyze the data used to support this argument in terms of the following hypothesis: Physical illness, especially during the beginning phases, can cause a major life change.

4. The text outlined the responses to stress in terms of the general adaptation syndrome. Consider the last time you suffered from a relatively major illness. Can you identify the role of stress in leading to this illness? Did the problem proceed in the stages suggested by the general adaptation syndrome?

Personality: Theories and Assessment

CHAPTER OUTLINE

After completing Chapter 11, you should:

1. Understand what Eric Sevareid meant when he said that chance may have put Truman in the presidential post, but his character or personality "kept him there and determined his historical fate."

2. Be aware that situational consistency and situational variation represent two extremes descriptions of personality and that the "truth" lies somewhere in between these extremes.

3. Be able to contrast type and trait approaches to personality, particularly the advantages and disadvantages and disadvantages of each approach.

4. Realize that Freud placed a great deal of emphasis on the influence of the unconscious on personality and its development.

5. Be able to contrast the roles of id, ego, and superego in determining a person's behavior.

6. Know the highlights of Freud's stages of personality development and understand why the events that are supposed to occur during the Phallic Stage have been questioned by contemporary psychologists.

7. Be able to discuss the Neo-Freudians in terms of the heritage they share with Freud *and* the sometimes dramatic departures they made from his theory.

8. Be able to list the characteristics that humanistic theories like those of Maslow and Rogers have in common.

9. Understand why Rogers felt that unconditional positive regard was such an essential part of his "client-centered" therapy.

10. Realize that Skinner and the humanists represent two opposite extremes in their approaches to the role of the "self" in personality development.

11. Be able to contrast social learning theory with Skinner's approach to personality.

12. Know how observational or cognitive learning is different from trial-and-error learning.

13. Understand why the statement "The buck stops here" probably was made by someone with an *internal* locus of control.

14. Be aware that the personality theory one accepts has serious consequences for the direction of research one pursues.

15. Be able to contrast test reliability with test validity and see why both are necessary.

16. Be able to compare and contrast the advantages and disadvantages of behavioral assessment, interviews, questionnaires, and projective tests.

17. See how interviews and questionnaires share many of the same drawbacks because they are both rather "direct" methods of personality assessment.

18. See why projective tests are a natural extension of Freud's theoretical position.

KEY TERMS SELF-TEST

In each group below, fill in the letter of the term on the right with the appropriate definition on the left.

Personality: Types and Traits

Definitions

1. the unique set of behaviors and enduring qualities that influence a person's adjustment to the environment

2. a person's body build

3. fairly permanent qualities that people possess to a greater or lesser degree

Key Terms

a. somatotype (p. 349)
b. personality (p. 346)
c. traits (p. 350)

Psychoanalytic Theory

Definitions

1. Freud's method of having patients express every thought that came into their heads

2. part of the personality made up of instinctual drives

3. part of the personality which works to control the impulses of the id

4. part of the personality representing our conscience

Key Terms

a. superego (p. 355)
b. reality principle (p. 354)
c. id (p. 354)
d. ego (p. 354)
e. pleasure principle (p. 354)
f. free association (p. 352)
g. libido (p. 354)

 5. the immediate satisfaction of drives without regard to reality, logic, or manners

 6. tries to satisfy the desires of the id by taking into account the possibilities of reward and punishment

 7. energy force that propels people to satisfy the drive for survival

Humanistic and Learning Theories

Definitions

Key Terms

 1. personality theory accepting that people are basically good and worthy of respect and stressing the achievement of potential

 2. process by which a person strives to learn, create, and work to the best of his or her ability

 3. fleeting moments in people's lives where they feel truly spontaneous and unconcerned with time or other physical constraints

 4. when the therapist accepts and cares for the client no matter what feelings or behaviors are revealed

 5. acquisition of knowledge and behavior by watching other people act and then doing the same thing

 6. learning by watching other people and observing the consequences of their actions

7. general expectancy concerning the source of control of what happens to a person

a. unconditional positive regard (p. 363)
b. self-actualization (p. 362)
c. locus of control (p. 368)
d. imitation (p. 366)
e. humanistic theory (p. 361)
f. peak experiences (p. 362)
g. cognitive learning or observational learning (p. 366)

Definitions

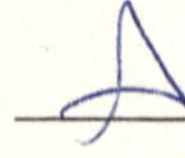

1. assessment by means of examining a person's present behavior to predict future actions

2. assessment technique that involves direct questioning of a person

3. personality questionnaire designed to identify specific psychological disorders

4. assessment technique based on Freud's theory that people will project unconscious desires onto ambiguous and nonthreatening stimuli

5. means that you get the same results on a test every time you administer it

6. means that the test actually measures what you say it measures

Key Terms

a. interview (p. 372)
b. reliability of a test (p. 371)
c. validity of a test (p. 371)
d. projective test (p. 375)
e. Minnesota Multiphasic Personality Inventory (p. 373)
f. behavioral assessment (p. 371)

Answers to Key Terms Self-Test

Personality: Types and Traits
1. b
2. a
3. c

Psychoanalytic Theory
1. f   5. e
2. c   6. b
3. d   7. g
4. a

Humanistic and Learning Theories
1. e   5. d
2. b   6. g
3. f   7. c
4. a

Personality Assessment
1. f   4. d
2. a   5. b
3. e   6. c

PRACTICE TESTS

Circle the correct letter.

1. A major focus of personality research is (p. 346):
   a. intrapsychic deviations.
   b. similarities between people.
   c. individual differences.
   d. group dynamics.

2. A classic study of children's moral behavior in a variety of situations indicated that (p. 346):
   a. there is a high degree of situational consistency in children's moral behavior.
   b. there was only a slight tendency for children who were dishonest in one setting to be dishonest in other settings.
   c. children who were dishonest in one setting were dishonest in all of the other settings.
   d. a and c above.

3. Bem and Allen's (1974) study of situational consistency along the friendly/unfriendly dimension showed that (p. 348):
   a. subjects who rated themselves as consistently friendly did, in fact, respond in a friendly manner in a variety of situations.
   b. subjects who rated themselves as consistently friendly were not consistent in this trait.
   c. subjects always rated themselves as consistently friendly.
   d. none of the above.

4. A basic assumption of the science of phrenology is that (p. 348):
   a. there is not any connection between physical appearance and personality.
   b. personality is determined by situational factors.
   c. personality involves an interaction between heredity and environment.
   d. personality can be determined by examining the physical formation of the skull.

5. According to Sheldon, individuals with a mesomorphic body build or somatotype (p. 349):
   a. are muscular, hard, and rectangular.
   b. are assertive, physical, aggressive, and active.
   c. are tall, thin, and fragile.
   d. a and b above.

6. Sheldon's type theory can be criticized because (p. 350):
   a. the relationship between body build and personality is *simpler* than Sheldon suggested.
   b. our *expectations* about how people with certain body types should behave may have a greater influence than the body types themselves.
   c. people can be categorized more easily than Sheldon thought.
   d. there is no relationship between personality and body type.

7. Trait theories of personality (pp. 350-351):
    a. *only* let us classify people as either having a characteristic or not having it.
    b. allow us to rate how much of a certain trait an individual possesses.
    c. have an advantage over type theories because of the limited number of traits one would need to consider.
    d. a and c above.

8. Trait theories can be criticized on the grounds that (pp. 351-352):
    a. they can lead to circular reasoning.
    b. they do not pay enough attention to the influence of the situation on behavior.
    c. they do not tell us how personality develops or changes.
    d. all of the above.

9. The major focus of psychoanalytic theory is (p. 352):
    a. on the influence of traits on behavior.
    b. on the influence of situations on behavior.
    c. on the development of personality.
    d. on the influence of somatotypes on personality.

10. Freud's discussion with middle- and upper-class women led him to the conclusion that (pp. 352-353):
    a. early childhood is a critical time for the formation of personality.
    b. children, even infants, have sexual urges.
    c. hypnosis is the perfect tool for uncovering events related to hysterical symptoms.
    d. a and b above.

11. According to Freud, the _____________________ includes thoughts that people may not be aware of but which they can retrieve from memory (p. 353):
    a. preconscious
    b. conscious
    c. unconscious
    d. alter conscious

12. According to Freud, threatening impulses are (p. 353):
    a. repressed, but can still influence behavior.
    b. forced into the preconscious.
    c. expressed in their original form.
    d. repressed, and can never influence behavior.

13. According to Freud, Eros is (p. 354):
    a. a destructive drive.
    b. the drive for survival.
    c. a drive including the needs to eat, drink, be warm, and engage in sexual activity.
    d. b and c above.

14. In Freud's theory, the ego (p. 354):
    a. is concerned with moral and ethical aspects of actions.
    b. is concerned only about the consequences of actions.
    c. operates at the unconscious level.
    d. operates according to the pleasure principle.

15. Freud would most likely argue that someone who smokes excessively (p. 356):
    a. was fixated at the oral stage.
    b. was probably an unhappy adolescent.
    c. was improperly toilet trained.
    d. had an Oedipal complex.

16. The anal retentive personality (p. 357):
    a. is an aggressive, sadistic person.
    b. is rebellious and very messy.
    c. is compulsively neat and orderly.
    d. spends a large amount of time talking or singing.

17. During the phallic stage, the young female (p. 358):
    a. goes through the Oedipus complex.
    b. may envy her father's penis.
    c. goes through the Electra complex.
    d. b and c above.

18. Carl Jung, a neo-Freudian, believed that people adopt one of two basic approaches to the world. They are (p. 359):
    a. basic anxiety and basic hostility.
    b. feelings of superiority and feelings of inferiority.
    c. introversion and extroversion.
    d. mastery and competence.

19. According to Karen Horney (pp. 359-360):
    a. women may envy the status that society has given men.
    b. women envy men's penises.
    c. penis envy is the basis for the "castrating female" personality.
    d. b and c above.

20. Adler developed the concept of ______________________ to explain why certain people born with organ defects develop a life style to compensate for these defects (p. 360):
    a. organ compensation
    b. compensatory athletics
    c. organ inferiority
    d. none of the above.

21. Maslow argued that (pp. 361-362):
    a. humans have a natural motivation to be creative and reach their highest potential.
    b. highest potential cannot be achieved until more basic needs have been met.
    c. human needs are arranged in a hierarchy.
    d. all of the above.

22. Which of the following orderings of Maslow's hierarchy of needs is correct (p. 361)?
    a. basic necessities, personal safety, meta needs.
    b. personal safety, basic necessities, meta needs.
    c. meta needs, personal safety, basic necessities.
    d. meta needs, basic necessities, personal safety.

23. According to Maslow, individuals like Abraham Lincoln or Eleanor Roosevelt were (p. 362):
    a. peak individuals.
    b. self-confident.
    c. self-actualized.
    d. self-important.

24. Carl Rogers was instrumental in developing (p. 364):
    a. client-centered therapy.
    b. gestalt therapy.
    c. dynamic therapy.
    d. behavior therapy.

25. According to Carl Rogers, the self-concept (p. 362):
    a. develops by acceptance of certain values and rejection of others.
    b. has no influence on how we act or perceive our world.
    c. need not include an honest representation, but must include what society finds acceptable.
    d. would only be hurt by unconditional positive regard.

26. Which of the following is *not* a valid criticism of humanistic theories (p. 364)?
    a. Humanists have failed to clearly define the important terms of their theories.
    b. Such a broad view is taken that it is difficult to make predictions about behavior in specific situations.
    c. They show too much concern for people's integrity and uniqueness.
    d. Humanists rely on too few concepts to explain the complexity of human behavior.

27. Learning theories of personality (pp. 364-365):
    a. emphasize "internal forces" in their explanations of behavior.
    b. assume behavior can be explained by looking at environmental conditions.
    c. assume behavior can be explained by looking at rewards and punishments.
    d. b and c above.

28. Which of the following is *not* true about Skinner's approach to personality (p. 365)?
    a. Skinner believes that the environment determines an individual's behavior.
    b. Skinner rejects the idea that people have "free will."
    c. Skinner believes that individual differences are the result of genetic variations.
    d. Skinner believes an ideal society can be created using the principles of behavior
        modification.

29. Social learning theorists (pp. 365-366):
    a. deny that external rewards and punishments play a role in personality.
    b. believe trial-and-error learning is the *only* kind of learning.
    c. believe we learn more than behavior; we also learn rules, languages, and expectancies.
    d. deny personal or internal influences on behavior.

30. Social learning theorists believe that observational or cognitive learning can occur (p. 366):
    a. for only a limited number of behaviors.
    b. without external reinforcement.
    c. without actually performing the behavior.
    d. b and c above.

31. Children who saw a model rewarded for aggressively attacking a Bobo doll (p. 367):
    a. *learned* more aggressive behavior than children who saw the model unrewarded or punished.
    b. acted more aggressively toward the Bobo doll than children who saw the model unrewarded
        or punished.
    c. acted less aggressively toward the Bobo doll than children who saw the model unrewarded
        or punished.
    d. none of the above.

32. According to Mischel competencies, encoding strategies, expectancies, subjective values, and
    self-regulatory systems are (p. 367):
    a. reward contingencies.
    b. imitative strategies.
    c. person variables that influence behavior and account for why people in the same situation
        respond differently.
    d. task variables.

33. People with an internal locus of control (p. 368):
    a. believe they control their own fate.
    b. feel responsible for the results of their behavior.
    c. believe what happens to them is the result of luck or chance.
    d. a and b above.

34. People with an external locus of control (p. 368):
    a. believe their failures are due to task difficulty or bad luck.
    b. believe their failures are due to their own lack of ability.
    c. believe their failures are due to their own lack of effort.
    d. feel more shame for their failures than people with an internal locus of control.

35. Suppose you have just completed a college entrance exam. You have scored quite low on the
    test. However, you believe you would do very well in college if you were admitted. You might
    question the test's (p. 371):
    a. reliability.
    b. criteria.
    c. validity.
    d. structure.

36. The natural observation method is an example of (p. 371):
    a. a projective test.
    b. behavioral assessment.
    c. indirect assessment.
    d. an interview technique.

37. Suppose an interviewer begins with planned questions but later questions are determined by
    the subject's responses. The interviewer is using a(n) (p. 372):
    a. questionnaire technique.
    b. structured interview.
    c. unstructured interview.
    d. projective test.

38. Which of the following is (are) drawbacks of the interview method of assessing personality
    (pp. 372-373)?
    a. People may be reluctant to present themselves in a bad light.
    b. Responses can be affected by the individual's feelings about the interviewer.
    c. Interviews can be very time-consuming.
    d. all of the above.

39. Which of the following is a common problem with questionnaires as an assessment technique
    (p. 373)?
    a. response bias
    b. indiscriminate learning
    c. regression towards the mean
    d. disgraphia

40. The Rorschach Inkblot Test is an example of (p. 375):
    a. a questionnaire.
    b. an interview.
    c. a projective test.
    d. natural observation.

1. c	11. a	21. d	31. b
2. b	12. a	22. a	32. c
3. a	13. d	23. c	33. d
4. d	14. b	24. a	34. a
5. d	15. a	25. a	35. c
6. b	16. c	26. c	36. b
7. b	17. d	27. d	37. c
8. d	18. c	28. c	38. d
9. c	19. a	29. c	39. a
10. d	20. c	30. d	40. c

THOUGHT QUESTIONS/APPLICATIONS

1. Sheldon argued that a person's body "type" influenced that person's personality characteristics. However, as your authors pointed out, our *expectations* of how thin, fat, or muscular individuals should behave may influence their behavior more than their body types *per se.* Can you think of other personality "types" that influence our expectations of people's behavior? If your immediate answer is "no," think more closely about the categories you might use for classifying new acquaintances (for example, "jock," "preppie," and so forth).

2. Suppose Freud's clients had been modern day women rather than Victorian women. How might his theory have differed? Would his emphasis on unconscious drives and sexual urges been as great with modern women?

3. One advantage of learning approaches to personality is that they are easy to test empirically. In contrast, the concepts of Humanistic approaches to personality tend to be difficult to define much less test experimentally. Suppose you were interested in testing Rogers' hypothesis that unconditional positive regard aids individuals in their development of a good self-concept. Try to devise an experimental test of this hypothesis.

4. Suppose you are interested in identifying individuals with internal and external loci of control. However, you do not want to use a questionnaire procedure to measure locus of control. How might natural observation or projective tests be adapted to measure this aspect of personality?

Abnormal Psychology

CHAPTER OUTLINE

Schizophrenia: Normal Adjustment to an Abnormal World?

CHAPTER OBJECTIVES

After reading Chapter 12, you should:

1. Understand why Charles Manson's behavior represents a "cafeteria" of psychological disorders and why no single diagnostic label captures the scope of his abnormalities.

2. Be able to explain why the statistical definition of abnormality is not sufficient for dealing with psychological disorders.

3. Realize that labeling a person as "abnormal" can be dangerous.

4. Be able to contrast the different models of abnormality (medical, psychoanalytic, learning, cognitive, and systems).

5. Be aware of the "medical student syndrome" and how it might affect the psychology student who is first learning about different psychological disorders.

6. Know the symptoms and prognosis of the two childhood disorders discussed in the text, infantile autism and anorexia nervosa.

7. Be able to distinguish between generalized anxiety disorder and phobias.

8. Know the difference between an obsession and a compulsion and why the two abnormalities often occur together.

9. Realize that people suffering from somatoform disorders are *not* faking their discomfort; they really "feel" it.

10. Know why conversion disorders are easy for doctors to distinguish from real organic disorders—particularly when the conversion symptom is paralysis of part of a limb (as in "glove anesthesia").

11. Know the different ways people have of "tuning out" difficult feelings or situations.

12. Be able to discuss both psychoanalytic and learning theories of depression. How might accepting one theory affect the treatment one provides for the depressed person?

13. Know the difference between gender identity disorder and transsexualism and how the former might progress into the latter.

14. Be able to list the major symptoms of schizophrenia, including disorganized thought, disorganized perception, disturbed communication, inappropriate emotions, and unusual motor activities.

15. Understand why it is so difficult to prove the link between genetic inheritance and schizophrenia.

16. Be able to explain Laing's belief that schizophrenia is a normal adjustment to an abnormal world. What might be wrong with this belief?

17. Know the difference between drug use and drug addiction. Also, be aware that individuals can become *psychologically* dependent on drugs as well as physically dependent.

KEY TERMS SELF-TEST

In each group below, fill in the letter of the term on the right with the appropriate definition on the left.

Abnormal Behavior, Childhood Disorders, and Anxiety Disorders

Definitions

Key Terms

________ 1. behavior that is unusual, causes distress to others, and/or makes it difficult for a person to adjust to the environment

________ 2. one of the most commonly used systems for classifying abnormal behavior

________ 3. disorder in which infants withdraw, do not react to others, and become attached to inanimate objects

a. neurosis (p. 395)
b. abnormal behavior (p. 384)
c. phobia (p. 396)
d. generalized anxiety disorder (p. 395)
e. anorexia nervosa (p. 394)
f. infantile autism (p. 392)
g. DSM III (Diagnostic and Statistical Manual) (p. 385)
h. obsessive-compulsive disorder (p. 397)

4. a condition in which a person loses
   appetite, eats little, and slowly
   starves

5. a broad pattern of disorders
   characterized by anxiety, fear,
   and self-defeating behaviors

6. disorder in which people experience
   overwhelming anxiety, but cannot
   identify its source

7. irrational fear of a specific object
   or event

8. irrational, recurring thought or
   behavior that cannot be
   controlled

Somatoform Disorders and Dissociative Disorders

Definitions

1. group of disorders in which people
   show physical symptoms but there
   is no sign of organic damage

2. specific disorder characterized by
   vague but dramatic complaints

3. specific somatoform disorder
   involving one specific symptom
   (for example, paralysis of a limb)

4. group of disorders characterized by
   "tuning out" a part of the person
   from the situation at hand

5. selective forgetting of past events

6. disorder involving loss of memory
   and physical flight

7. disorder in which one person assumes
   two or more personalities

Key Terms

a. somatoform disorders (p. 398)
b. dissociative disorders (p. 400)
c. multiple personalities (p. 401)
d. conversion disorders (p. 399)
e. somatization disorder (p. 399)
f. amnesia (p. 400)
g. fugue (p. 400)

Definitions

                  Key Terms

_C_ 1. group of disorders involving problems with emotions and moods

_D_ 2. disorder in which there is a loss of interest in most activities

_B_ 3. disorder in which person alternates between manic and depressive stages

_E_ 4. disorder in which males are unable to to have an erection or maintain one

_F_ 5. disorder in which females experience pain during intercourse

_A_ 6. disorder in which involuntary tightening of the vagina makes intercourse impossible

a. vaginismus (p. 408)
b. bipolar disorder (p. 406)
c. affective disorder (p. 401)
d. depression (p. 401)
e. impotence (p. 408)
f. dyspareunia (p. 408)

Other Disorders

Definitions

                  Key Terms

_B_ 1. disturbances caused by unresolved conflicts so great that the person can no longer deal with reality

_D_ 2. disorders characterized by disorganization of thoughts, perceptions, communication, and motor behavior

_C_ 3. rigid and maladaptive ways of dealing with the environment

_A_ 4. disorder in which people perform violent acts without any regret or guilt

a. antisocial personality (p. 417)
b. psychoses (p. 409)
c. personality disorders (p. 416)
d. schizophrenia (p. 409)

Abnormal Behavior, Childhood Disorders, and Anxiety Disorders

1. b	5. a
2. g	6. d
3. f	7. c
4. e	8. h

Affective Disorders, Bipolar Disorders, and Sexual Disorders

1. c	4. e
2. d	5. f
3. b	6. a

Somatoform Disorders and Dissociative Disorders

1. a	5. f
2. e	6. g
3. d	7. c
4. b	

Other Disorders

1. b
2. d
3. c
4. a

PRACTICE TEST

Circle the correct letter.

1. The "statistical" definition of abnormality (p. 384):
   a. defines abnormal behavior in terms of deviations from average behavior.
   b. excludes outstandingly *good* behavior.
   c. takes cultural differences into account.
   d. carefully considers the consequences of abnormal behaviors.

2. The president's commission on mental health estimated that _______________ percent of the population suffers from mild to moderate depression and other emotional disorders (p. 385):
   a. 5
   b. 10
   c. 25
   d. 50

3. The Diagnostic and Statistical Manual (DSM III) focuses on (p. 385):
   a. organic causes of disorders.
   b. interpretation of disorders.
   c. treatment of disorders.
   d. symptoms of disorders.

4. The "M'Naghten" rule (p. 386);
    a. became the legal standard for defining insanity.
    b. held that someone must know right from wrong at the time of a crime in order to be held
        responsible for that crime.
    c. is presently used in the United States in its original form.
    d. both a and b above.

5. The rule which states that a person is not responsible for an act committed while "as a result
   of a mental disease or defect, he lacks substantial capacity to appreciate the wrongfulness of
   his conduct or to conform his conduct to the requirements of the law" is called (p. 386):
    a. the M'Naghten rule.
    b. the Brawner rule.
    c. the legal insanity rule.
    d. the O'Shea rule.

6. When one's expectations cause to happen what one expects to happen, we have (p. 387):
    a. the exception rather than the rule.
    b. self-fulfilling prophecy.
    c. self-perpetuating labels.
    d. none of the above.

7. When perfectly normal individuals admitted themselves to psychiatric hospitals complaining of
   hearing "voices," (pp. 387-388):
    a. the ruse was immediately detected and the pseudopatients were asked to leave.
    b. the hospital staffs had difficulty labeling the pseudopatients' disorders.
    c. even the normal behavior of the pseudopatients was interpreted as abnormal by hospital
        staff.
    d. although the hospital staffs were initially "fooled," they soon discovered they were being
        deceived and asked the pseudopatients to leave.

8. Cultures believing that abnormal behavior is caused by possession by spirits (pp. 388-389):
    a. always tortured the possessed person.
    b. tortured the possessed person when they believed evil spirits were responsible for the
        possession.
    c. honored the possessed person when they believed good spirits were responsible for the
        possession.
    d. both b and c above.

9. The "medical model" of abnormal behavior can be criticized because (p. 389):
    a. it is sometimes impossible to identify biological causes of disorders.
    b. the medical definition of abnormal behavior is based on social norms that can change
        over time.
    c. it may be demeaning to label someone as mentally sick.
    d. all of the above.

10. The _________________________ model of abnormal behavior focuses on early childhood and
    argues that abnormal behavior is the result of unresolved conflicts (p. 390).
    a. psychoanalytic
    b. learning
    c. cognitive
    d. systems

11. The _________________________ model of abnormal behavior views abnormal behavior and
    normal behavior similarly; both are learned in the same way (p. 390).
    a. psychoanalytic
    b. learning
    c. cognitive
    d. systems

12. The main difference between learning and cognitive approaches to abnormal behavior is
    (p. 390):
    a. the learning approach involves retraining but the cognitive approach does not.
    b. the cognitive approach involves retraining but the learning approach does not.
    c. the cognitive approach accepts the medical model, but the learning approach does not.
    d. the learning approach works directly with behavior while the cognitive approach works on
       teaching the person new attitudes or beliefs.

13. A researcher who argues that certain psychological disorders are often associated with certain

    social settings probably accepts the _________________________ model of abnormal behavior
    (p. 391).
    a. systems
    b. psychoanalytic
    c. learning
    d. cognitive

14. Joan is a first-year psychology major. She has been reading about bipolar disorders. She realizes
    that she has periods of great excitement and periods of depression. In panic, she concludes that
    she is suffering from a bipolar disorder. Joan is actually suffering from (p. 392):
    a. severe depression.
    b. an affective disorder.
    c. the "medical student syndrome."
    d. anorexia nervosa.

15. Childhood disorders occur with the greatest frequency (p. 392):
    a. between 6 months and 3 years.
    b. during early adolescence.
    c. both a and b above.
    d. neither of the above.

16. Infantile autism (pp. 393-394):
    a. usually begins during the first year of life.
    b. has an excellent prognosis.
    c. occurs more often in boys than in girls.
    d. usually begins after age 4.

17. According to Casper and Davis, the first phase of anorexia nervosa involves (p. 394):
    a. an intense fear that eating will make the individual fat.
    b. low self-esteem and an increasing concern for physical appearance.
    c. extreme weight loss.
    d. admission that they have lost too much weight.

18. Neurotic behavior (p. 395):
    a. is maladaptive behavior aimed at dealing with anxiety.
    b. does not allow the person to completely control anxiety.
    c. keeps the person from developing effective ways of reducing anxiety.
    d. all of the above.

19. People who become highly agitated in the absence of any known cause can be said to suffer from (p. 395-396):
    a. obsessive-compulsive disorders.
    b. phobias.
    c. generalized anxiety disorder.
    d. somatoform disorders.

20. People with phobias (pp. 396-397):
    a. recognize the irrationality of their fear in most cases.
    b. are more likely to be men than women.
    c. tend to be of below average intelligence.
    d. tend to suffer from disorders in addition to their phobias.

21. In her repetitive hand-washing, Lady Macbeth was displaying (p. 398):
    a. a somatoform disorder.
    b. an anxiety disorder.
    c. an obsessive-compulsive disorder.
    d. both b and c above.

22. Mary has been to the doctor numerous times throughout her life. She complains of vague but dramatic discomforts. Her doctor can find no organic problem. Mary (p. 399):
    a. is "faking."
    b. is suffering from a somatization disorder.
    c. is suffering from a conversion disorder.
    d. is suffering from a dissociative disorder.

23. Conversion disorders (p. 399):
    a. involve many vague symptoms.
    b. involve symptoms that make perfect anatomical sense.
    c. often appear shortly after some stressful event and have sudden onsets.
    d. are associated with symptoms that persist even when people are asleep or hypnotized.

24. A person suffering from a dissociative disorder (p. 400):
    a. may be trying to repress unwanted thoughts or urges.
    b. has total control over onset of the disorder.
    c. tunes out part of himself or herself from the situation at hand.
    d. both a and c above.

25. Jane Doe is found wandering around the streets of a major city, very dazed. She does not know
    who she is. Apparently she lost her memory and fled following some difficulty at home. Jane
    Doe is suffering from (p. 400):
    a. simple amnesia.
    b. psychogenic fugue.
    c. somnambulism.
    d. multiple personality disorder.

26. People are most likely to attempt suicide (pp. 402-403):
    a. when they are in the grip of a depressive episode.
    b. if they have been talking about committing sucide.
    c. when they are coming out of a depressive episode.
    d. both b and c above.

27. A general and deep depression is most likely to occur (p. 404):
    a. if they attribute lack of control to the situation they are in.
    b. if they attribute lack of control to their own lack of ability.
    c. if they attribute lack of control to others.
    d. none of the above.

28. Boys who shun playing with other boys, develop female gestures, and engage solely in female
    play activities are suffering from (p. 407):
    a. gender identity disorder.
    b. transsexualism.
    c. homosexualism.
    d. childhood schizophrenia.

29. Which of the following is *not* a symptom of schizophrenia (pp. 410-412)?
    a. disorganization of thought
    b. hallucinations
    c. performance of violent acts without guilt or remorse
    d. inappropriate emotions

30. A "double-bind" conflict (p. 417):
    a. results when children receive contradictory messages from their parents.
    b. can contribute to the development of schizophrenia.
    c. both a and b above.
    d. none of the above.

31. R. D. Laing, a humanistic psychologist, believes that schizophrenia (p. 418):
    a. may be an attempt to adjust to a "crazy" world.
    b. is really an invention of psychiatrists.
    c. is a label that should not be used.
    d. is totally determined by genes.

32. People with antisocial personality disorders (p. 419):
    a. perform violent acts, but then show remorse for them.
    b. are incapable of forming close relationships with others.
    c. are manipulative and insincere.
    d. both b and c above.

33. The "problem drinker" (p. 420):
    a. is addicted to alcohol.
    b. often drinks too much and drinking for them has undesirable effects.
    c. has an increasing tolerance to alcohol and so must continue to increase the dosage.
    d. is indistinguishable from the alcoholic.

34. Physical dependence on drugs develops from (p. 421):
    a. narcotics and amphetamines.
    b. barbiturates and nicotine.
    c. hallucinogens.
    d. both a and b above.

35. When a person stops taking a drug that he or she was psychologically dependent upon, the person (p. 422):
    a. experiences physical pain much like withdrawal from drugs involving physical dependence.
    b. may experience anxiety, depression, and uneasiness.
    c. does not experience any bad effects.
    d. none of the above.

1. a	11. b	21. d	31. a
2. c	12. d	22. b	32. d
3. d	13. a	23. c	33. b
4. d	14. c	24. d	34. d
5. b	15. c	25. b	35. b
6. b	16. a	26. d	
7. c	17. b	27. b	
8. d	18. d	28. a	
9. d	19. c	29. c	
10. a	20. a	30. c	

THOUGHT QUESTIONS/APPLICATIONS

1. Think carefully about your own behavior. Clearly, everyone has thoughts, feelings, or behaviors which resemble some of the symptoms of the psychological disorders discussed in Chapter 12. However, you are probably *not* suffering from any of the serious psychological disorders discussed in the chapter. Given the definition of abnormality on pages 384 and 385, what makes your behavior well within the "normal" range?

2. In this chapter, great emphasis was placed on classifying abnormal behavior. "Symptoms" of various disorders were described in detail. When this approach to abnormality is taken, there is a danger of labeling a person's problem and then thinking you understand it. How might this labeling interfere with successful treatment of someone's psychological problems?

3. R. D. Laing has suggested that schizophrenia reflects normal adjustment to a "crazy" world. Could this interpretation be made of any of the other disorders discussed in Chapter 12?

4. The chapter was divided into several major classification headings, including neurosis, somatoform disorders, and psychosis. Under each heading, different disorders that were "similar" in some way were listed. Were the differences between disorders under different headings really *greater* than the differences between disorders under the same heading? For example, are dissociative and affective disorders more similar than dissociative disorders and anxiety disorders? Why or why not?

13

Therapy

CHAPTER OUTLINE

Aversive conditioning
Systematic desensitization
Operant conditioning therapies
Modeling

Group Therapies
Family Therapy
Community Psychology
Personal Growth Techniques

Transpersonal psychology
T-groups and encounter groups

Does Psychotherapy Work?

CHAPTER OBJECTIVES

After completing Chapter 13, you should:

1. Be able to discuss Chris Costner's emotional problems in terms of the many different approaches to therapy presented in the chapter.

2. Be familiar with the historical background of psychotherapy and how it reflects links between our beliefs concerning the causes of psychological disorders and the way in which we treat those disorders.

3. Know the six different types of therapists and how they differ in terms of training and responsibilities.

4. Realize that many forms of biotherapy were developed because of accidental discoveries, not because of careful exploration of the causes of psychological disorders.

5. Be able to weigh the pros and cons of electroconvulsive therapy and know when its use is most appropriate.

6. Understand why medical professionals are much less likely to resort to prefrontal lobotomies today than they were during the 1940s and 1950s.

7. Be able to list the major categories of drugs used to treat psychological disorders and know which disorders are most aided by each type of drug.

8. Be acutely aware that the benefits of chemotherapy are associated with some serious risks.

9. Be able to discuss one way of helping people control their physiological functions without the use of drugs.

10. Know the major techniques used by psychoanalysts in treating anxiety disorders.

11. Be able to compare and contrast client-centered therapy and gestalt therapy, highlighting their similarities.

12. Be able to see how rational emotive therapy is aimed at changing people's thoughts while behavior therapies are aimed at changing their external behaviors.

13. Know the differences among aversive conditioning therapy, systematic desensitization, and operant conditioning therapies. What drawbacks might we face in using these behavior therapies?

14. Understand the advantages and disadvantages of group therapies and be able to explain why they are not always used.

15. Understand why a family therapy approach may be particularly useful when dealing with adolescents and their emotional problems.

16. Know what professionals can do on the community level to promote mental health.

17. Know the difference between t-groups and encounter groups and understand why it is essential that these groups be led by competent professionals.

18. Be aware that answering the question of whether psychotherapy works is not as simple as it seems.

KEY TERMS SELF-TEST

In each group below, fill in the letter of the term on the right with the appropriate definition on the left.

Biotherapy

Definitions   Key Terms

_____ c   1. the use of drugs, surgery, or electric   a. electroconvulsive therapy (p. 432)
               shock to induce behavior change   b. chemotherapy (p. 434)
                                                                c. biotherapy (p. 428)
_____ a   2. technique in which electric shock is   d. psychosurgery (p. 434)
               administered to patient's brain,   e. prefrontal lobotomy (p. 434)
               causing convulsions   f. biofeedback (p. 436)

_____ d   3. biotherapy techniques involving
               surgery on the brain

4. surgical technique in which connections between thalamus and frontal lobes are cut

5. treatment of disorders through the use of drugs

6. technique that provides people with feedback on their physiological functions so they can learn to control these functions

Psychotherapy I

Definitions

1. the use of psychological techniques to help a client change his or her behavior

2. Freud's technique of treating anxiety disorders by helping people recognize and deal with repressed feelings

3. defense mechanism involving the blocking of unpleasant thoughts from conscious awareness

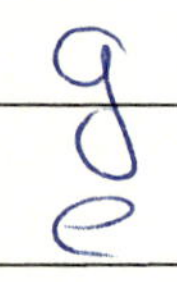

4. storehouse of unacceptable images according to Freud

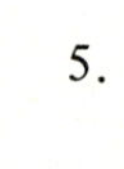

5. Freud's technique for helping clients understand the latent content of their dreams

6. Rogers' therapy approach aimed at providing the proper setting for self-growth

7. when the therapist accepts and cares for the client no matter what feelings or behaviors are revealed

Key Terms

a. client-centered therapy (p. 440)
b. psychotherapy (p. 438)
c. unconditional positive regard (p. 440)
d. psychoanalysis (p. 437)
e. dream interpretation (p. 438)
f. repression (p. 437)
g. unconscious (p. 437)

Psychotherapy II

Definitions

1. type of therapy in which person receives unpleasant consequences for undesired behavior

2. type of therapy in which clients are taught to use deep muscle relaxation when faced with feared or stressful events or objects

3. type of learning that occurs when desired responses are reinforced and undesired responses are ignored or punished

4. behavioral technique in which people are given tokens as rewards for performing desired behaviors

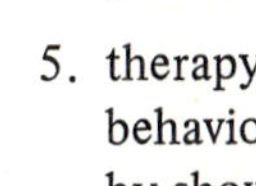
5. therapy technique to teach new behaviors or strengthen existing ones by showing a model behaving appropriately

Key Terms

a. aversive conditioning (p. 444)
b. operant conditioning (p. 445)
c. modeling (p. 447)
d. systematic desensitization (p. 444)
e. token economies (p. 445)

Psychotherapy III

Definitions

1. therapy in which clients receive feedback from others in a group as well as from the therapist

2. therapy that involves the whole family, rather than just one member of it

3. subfield of psychology dedicated to promoting mental health at the community level

4. technique for increasing people's self-awareness through a mixture of psychological theory, religion, and modern philosophy

Key Terms

a. T-group (p. 454)
b. community psychology (p. 451)
c. transpersonal psychology (p. 453)
d. family therapy (p. 450)
e. group therapy (p. 448)
f. encounter group/sensitivity group (p. 454)

5. type of group therapy focusing on how people function in groups rather than on emotional disorders

6. technique aimed at expanding personal awareness and growth rather than treating emotional disorders by trying to rid people of their interpersonal "hang-ups"

Answers to Key Terms Self-Test

Biotheraphy

1. c   4. e
2. a   5. b
3. d   6. f

Psychotherapy I

1. b   5. e
2. d   6. a
3. f   7. c
4. g

Psythotherapy II

1. a   4. e
2. d   5. c
3. b

Psychotherapy III

1. e   4. c
2. d   5. a
3. b   6. f

PRACTICE TEST

Circle the correct letter.

1. The basic goal(s) of all types of biotherapy and psychotherapy is (are) (p. 428):
   a. Do not bring harm or intensify.
   b. Reduce the individual's present discomfort.
   c. Aid in the development of a more adjusted individual.
   d. all of the above.

2. Psychologically disturbed individuals were beaten, burned, and so forth in ancient times because (p. 428):
   a. all disorders, physical and psychological, met with cruel treatment.
   b. people believed the maltreatment would destroy the "demons" possessing the disturbed individual.
   c. other, more humane treatments, did not work.
   d. none of the above.

162

3. In the early part of this century (p. 429):
    a. all therapists adopted a "Freudian" approach to treatment.
    b. biotherapy was totally unthinkable.
    c. psychotherapy was mainly individual therapy involving a single patient.
    d. group and family therapies were very popular.

4. Cerletti believed that electric shock helped to eliminate mental disease because (p. 430):
    a. it changed the patient's brain waves.
    b. it brought the patient close to death.
    c. it aroused the body's natural defenses.
    d. b and c above.

5. The only therapists who can prescribe drugs or conduct psychosurgery are (pp. 430-431):
    a. psychiatrists.
    b. psychiatric social workers.
    c. clinical psychologists.
    d. counseling psychologists.

6. A psychiatric social worker (p. 431):
    a. has special training in interviewing and may visit people in their homes.
    b. is usually involved with patient care.
    c. generally holds a Ph.D. and works with hospital patients.
    d. is often skilled at psychoanalytic techniques.

7. Most advances in biotherapy have been the result of (p. 432):
    a. a careful, concentrated effort to develop these cures.
    b. serendipity.
    c. theoretical work providing a firm answer to the question of why biotherapy works.
    d. both a and c above.

8. Electroconvulsive therapy (pp. 432-433):
    a. is extremely painful.
    b. frightens many people.
    c. causes convulsions similar to epileptic seizures.
    d. b and c above.

9. The benefits of electroconvulsive therapy (p. 433):
    a. are short-term.
    b. are limited to those suffering from depressive disorders.
    c. a and b above.
    d. are long-term and available for those suffering from a variety of psychological disorders.

10. Prefrontal lobotomies (p. 434):
    a. help reduce the intensity of people's emotions.
    b. were never used very extensively to treat psychological disorders.
    c. have few negative side effects.
    d. can always be undone if negative side effects do occur.

11. Valium, Librium, and Miltown are (p. 434):
    a. antidepressant drugs.
    b. antipsychotic drugs.
    c. antianxiety drugs.
    d. antiosociopathic drugs.

12. Antipsychotic drugs (p. 435):
    a. are used to calm and relieve delusions.
    b. may cause headaches and other negative side effects.
    c. may even result in brain damage with prolonged use.
    d. all of the above.

13. Lithium Carbonate (p. 435):
    a. is used to treat schizophrenia.
    b. is used to treat people with bipolar disorders.
    c. is one of the safest drugs currently used to treat psychological disorders.
    d. has been removed from the market because it is too dangerous.

14. Which of the following is *not* a valid criticism against the use of drugs in treating psychological disorders (p. 436)?
    a. They are used to bring peace to mental hospital wards, not to help the individual patient.
    b. They may only reduce the symptoms of disorders without dealing with underlying causes.
    c. Psychotherapy is always more effective than the use of drugs.
    d. Patients may become dependent on the drugs to make them "feel good."

15. ______________________________ is designed to help people control their physiological functions without the use of drugs (p. 436).
    a. Biofeedback therapy
    b. Chemotherapy
    c. Psychotherapy
    d. Group therapy

16. Which method was *not* used by Freud to identify repressed feelings (pp. 437-438)?
    a. role playing
    b. dream interpretation
    c. having a client talk about whatever came to mind
    d. free association

17. A man reports that in his dream he jumped off a tall building. Freud would call this the

______________________________ of the man's dream (p. 438).
   a. expressed content
   b. manifest content
   c. latent content
   d. both a and b above

18. A young woman has always disliked her brother. In a session with her psychoanalyst, the young woman acts as if she dislikes her therapist. Freud would call this (p. 438):
   a. free association.
   b. transference.
   c. interpretation.
   d. repression.

19. Psychoanalysis is most successful in treating (p. 438):
   a. schizophrenia.
   b. depression.
   c. anxiety.
   d. bipolar disorder.

20. According to the humanists, we experience anxiety because (p. 439):
   a. we try to live up to others' expectations.
   b. we lose touch with our own desires and feelings.
   c. a and b above.
   d. none of the above.

21. When the client determines what will be discussed, not the therapist, the type of therapy being used is called (p. 440):
   a. free therapy.
   b. client-centered therapy.
   c. sensitivity therapy.
   d. gestalt therapy.

22. Carl Rogers was the originator of (p. 439):
   a. biotherapy.
   b. client-centered therapy.
   c. gestalt therapy.
   d. prefrontal lobotomy.

23. Early in the day, you had a fight with your spouse. Now you find yourself angry with a slow shop clerk. According to Gestalt therapists attributing your anger to the clerk's incompetence can be described as (p. 440):
   a. background.
   b. role playing.
   c. figure.
   d. transference.

24. Perls emphasizes the use of first-person pronouns in his Gestalt therapy because he believes they (p. 441):
    a. help people develop greater self-awareness.
    b. help people take responsibility for their behavior and thoughts.
    c. a and b above.
    d. none of the above.

25. During therapy sessions, Laura is often asked to pretend she is her mother. Laura's therapist pretends to be Laura, and the two of them act out situations. This technique is known as (p. 441):
    a. the empty chair technique.
    b. transference.
    c. role play.
    d. projection.

26. Which of the following is *not* true about rational emotive therapy (p. 442)?
    a. The therapy is aimed at restructuring the way people think.
    b. Therapists should *not* take an active role in therapy.
    c. Therapists should point out irrational beliefs and suggest more rational ones.
    d. Therapists should *not* be overly concerned about establishing a warm, caring relationship with the client.

27. Which of the following types of therapists would be most likely to have the belief that maladaptive behavior is learned through the same process as adaptive behavior (p. 443)?
    a. rational emotive therapists
    b. client-centered therapists
    c. psychoanalytic therapists
    d. behavior therapists

28. When an undesirable behavior is associated with an unpleasant event, the therapist is using (p. 444):
    a. systematic desensitization.
    b. aversive conditioning therapy.
    c. token economy therapy.
    d. reverse conditioning therapy.

29. Which of the following is *not* a step in systematic desensitization (pp. 444-445)?
    a. Clients are given tokens for appropriate behaviors.
    b. Events or objects that cause stress are identified.
    c. Stressful events are arranged in a hierarchy.
    d. Clients are taught to pair deep muscle relaxation with stressful events.

30. Whenever Jill completes her homework in the evening, her mother gives her a poker chip.
    Jill may use the poker chips to "buy" the privilege of watching her favorite television shows.
    Jill's mother is using (p. 445):
    a. rational emotive therapy.
    b. a token economy.
    c. aversive conditioning.
    d. systematic desensitization.

31. Which of the following is *not* a criticism of token economies (p. 445)?
    a. The person who gives out tokens has a great deal of power.
    b. People learn to work only for rewards.
    c. When rewards are stopped, desired behaviors may stop also.
    d. People usually will not work for tokens alone.

32. Modeling is most effective in teaching new behaviors when (p. 448):
    a. the model is older than the child.
    b. the model is younger than the child.
    c. the model is more popular than the child.
    d. the model is similar to the child.

33. Which of the following is (are) the advantage(s) of group therapy (p. 449)?
    a. It is more economical than individual therapy.
    b. It provides a setting for practicing interpersonal behaviors.
    c. The individual comes to know he or she is not alone in having problems.
    d. all of the above.

34. Family therapy is concerned most with (p. 450):
    a. rules and roles.
    b. meaningful verbalizations.
    c. group potential.
    d. transpersonal transactions.

35. The ___________________________ movement studies how environments can be altered to
    reduce stress and promote mental health (p. 451).
    a. family therapy
    b. personal growth
    c. community psychology
    d. humanistic psychology

36. ___________________________ represents a mixture of psychological theory, religion, and
    modern philosophy (p. 453):
    a. Transpersonal psychology
    b. Community psychology
    c. Humanistic psychology
    d. Psychoanalysis

37. T-groups (p. 454):
   a. are used only with mentally disturbed individuals.
   b. are led by trainers who make observations about the process of the group.
   c. begin with a predetermined structure and assigned task.
   d. are inappropriate for use in industrial settings.

38. The major aim of the encounter group or sensitivity group is to (p. 454):
   a. help members examine the group process.
   b. give members insight into how groups operate.
   c. a and b above.
   d. to expand personal awareness and growth.

39. The "casualties" of encounter groups (p. 455):
   a. were people who suffered negative effects from participating in the groups.
   b. resulted because participants were often not selected properly.
   c. included 9 to 33 percent of group participants.
   d. all of the above.

40. The "placebo effect" probably occurs because (p. 456):
   a. "self-fulfilling prophecies" may be at work.
   b. people gain a feeling of control over their lives.
   c. people are motivated to justify the effort they have put into therapy by getting better.
   d. all of the above.

Answers to Practice Test

1. d	11. c	21. b	31. d
2. b	12. d	22. c	32. d
3. c	13. b	23. c	33. d
4. d	14. c	24. c	34. a
5. a	15. a	25. c	35. c
6. a	16. a	26. b	36. a
7. b	17. d	27. d	37. b
8. d	18. b	28. b	38. d
9. c	19. c	29. a	39. d
10. a	20. c	30. b	40. d

1. A young woman reports that she is terrified of open spaces. How might a psychoanalyst explain and treat her problem? A behavior therapist? A rational emotive therapist?

2. Suppose you have been under a great deal of pressure lately. You are tense and anxious. Your doctor suggests you begin taking one of the anti-anxiety drugs, such as Valium. What questions might you have before you agree to this treatment?

3. Suppose you have a friend who is very depressed. She begins going to a therapist to try to overcome this depression. She pays the therapist $50.00 an hour and visits her once a week. After a month of therapy, your friend reports that she has recovered from her depression. Would you necessarily conclude that her therapist's techniques are responsible for this rapid recovery?

4. Suppose you have a serious emotional problem that is interfering with your daily life. What type of therapist might you prefer to see? Why? Suppose your best friend had the same type of problem. Would he or she choose the same type of therapy? How do personality characteristics determine which type of therapy is most desirable for an individual?

14

Interpersonal Relations

CHAPTER OUTLINE

CHAPTER OBJECTIVES

After completing Chapter 14, you should:

1. Understand why two different observers could interpret Malcolm X's behavior in completely different ways, making different attributions about his intentions and personal characteristics.

2. Know the three components of attitudes and understand why attitudes are easy to develop but hard to change.

3. Know why parents may have one of the largest impacts on the development of attitudes in their children.

4. Be aware that advertisers manipulate aspects of the communicator and the message in trying to sell their products.

5. Be able to explain the difference between the "foot-in-the-door" and "door-in-the-face" techniques and why both techniques work.

6. Understand how cognitive dissonance is produced by exerting great amounts of effort, getting insufficient reward for our actions, or conceding to very mild threats. How is this dissonance resolved in those situations?

7. Know our bases for attributing people's actions to internal or external causes.

8. Unfortunately, our attributions regarding other people are not always accurate. Know the different biases we have in attributing personal characteristics.

9. Be aware of the potentially powerful influence of self-fulfilling prophecies and know the pattern which they follow.

10. Be able to list the many different "gateways" to friendship and interpersonal attraction. Be aware of the role random chance plays in the formation of friendships.

11. Know when "birds of a feather" do and do not "flock together."

12. Realize that "irrelevant" characteristics such as wearing eyeglasses, having body and facial hair of certain quantities or colors, and dressing in certain manners subtly influence the attributions we make about people.

13. Understand that the decision to help someone in distress is a complicated one and involves much more than noticing the person's dilemma.

14. Be able to explain why there may not be safety in numbers when it comes to aiding a person in distress.

15. Realize that victims will not always be grateful when help is offered and know why this is the case.

KEY TERMS SELF-TEST

In each group below, fill in the letter of the term on the right with the appropriate definition on the left.

Social Psychology and Attitudes

Definitions

Key Terms

 1. the scientific study of the way in which people are affected by social situations and social relations

 2. learned, relatively enduring feelings about objects, events, or issues

 3. persuasive technique that gets people to agree first to a small request, so that they are then more willing to agree to a second request

 4. persuasive technique based on the fact that people who at first refuse a large request are more likely to comply with a smaller request

 5. state that occurs when a person's attitudes, beliefs, and behaviors are in conflict

a. attitudes (p. 465)
b. cognitive dissonance (p. 472)
c. door-in-the-face technique (p. 471)
d. social psychology (p. 464)
e. foot-in-the-door technique (p. 471)

Social Perception

Definitions

Key Terms

 1. the process of inferring characteristics of people from their observable behavior

 2. attributing an attitude based only on a person's behavior, failing to give sufficient weight to the situation

a. primacy effect (p. 479)
b. self-fulfilling prophecy (p. 481)
c. fundamental attribution error (p. 478)
d. attribution (p. 476)

________ 3. the fact that people tend to base
             their impressions on what they hear
             first

________ 4. an expectation that leads one to
             behave in ways that will cause that
             expectation to come about

Answers to Key Terms Self-Test

Social Psychology and Attitudes

1. d   4. c
2. a   5. b
3. e

Social Perception

1. d   3. a
2. c   4. b

PRACTICE TEST

Circle the correct letter.

1. Kurt Lewin, a psychologist who wrote in the late 1930s (p. 464):
   a. believed that everyday behavior was not influenced very much by other people in the environment.
   b. believed we must study how people are affected by their social situations.
   c. was not in favor of a systemaitc or scientific approach.
   d. did not favor carefully controlled experiments.

2. Which of the following is *not* a component of attitudes (p. 465)?
   a. influence
   b. evaluation
   c. belief
   d. action

3. Parents have a powerful influence on the development of their children's attitudes because (pp. 465-466):
   a. they have control over the rewards and punishments of their children.
   b. they control information that reaches their children.
   c. children tend to believe their parents.
   d. all of the above.

4. One of the main reasons peers influence the development of attitudes is that (p. 466):
   a. they always present attitudes different from the child's parents.
   b. children respect their peers more than their parents.
   c. children are afraid of being rejected by their peers if they do not act and believe as they do.
   d. none of the above.

5. In Jethro's judgment, the concert was fun. This was his (p. 465):
   a. religion.
   b. value.
   c. belief.
   d. evaluation.

6. Research has clearly shown that (p. 467):
   a. the media influence our attitudes.
   b. the media are often our only source of information about events.
   c. television is clearly the most persuasive medium of influence.
   d. a and b above.

7. The "sleeper effect" refers to (pp. 468-469):
   a. the credibility of an agent of attitude change having no effect on people's opinions.
   b. the early advantage of a more credible communicator being reduced over time.
   c. the early advantage of a more credible communicator being enhanced over time.
   d. most changes in opinion not persisting over time.

8. The message that smoking causes painful illness is (pp. 470-471):
   a. effective because it creates great fear.
   b. effective because it creates moderate fear.
   c. ineffective because it creates low fear.
   d. ineffective because it makes people uncomfortable.

9. Mary's sorority asks Mary to devote 20 hours per week to organization of this year's pledge activities. Mary refuses. Her sisters then ask her if she would be a cochairperson of the committee, and devote only 5 hours per week. Mary agrees. The sorority sisters have used the

   ___________________________ technique to get Mary to help them (p. 471).
   a. foot-in-the-door
   b. double request
   c. door-in-the-face
   d. none of the above

10. When a television commercial uses an "average American family" to sell a product, the advertiser is relying on (p. 470):
    a. the "trustworthy communicator" technique.
    b. the "communicator similarity" technique.
    c. emotional appeals.
    d. fear appeals.

11. LaPiere took a Chinese couple on a tour of the United States during a period in our history
    when anti-Chinese feelings were common. He found that (p. 472):
    a. the couple were given full service even by hotel and restaurant operators who said they were
        against serving Chinese people.
    b. the couple were given full service only by operators who said they were in favor of serving
        Chinese people.
    c. most hotel and restaurant operators concealed their anti-Chinese feelings when asked about
        their attitudes toward serving Chinese people.
    d. anti-Chinese feelings were demonstrated openly in face-to-face meetings with Chinese
        customers.

12. According to the cognitive dissonance theory, playing "hard to get" and being unkind to one's
    suitor causes the suitor to (pp. 472-473):
    a. become discouraged.
    b. become more enamoured.
    c. view the relationship negatively.
    d. become less caring, thus attracting the person to the suitor's attention.

13. Based on the research of Aronson and Mills, we might predict that a group of fraternity pledges
    undergoing severe initiation rites (pp. 473-474):
    a. would become more committed to the fraternity than pledges undergoing mild initiation
        rites.
    b. would become less committed to the fraternity than pledges undergoing mild initiation
        rites.
    c. would give negative evaluations of other members of the fraternity and fraternity activities.
    d. both b and c above.

14. If subjects are asked to skip breakfast before coming to an experiment and then asked to rate
    how hungry they are, (p. 475):
    a. they will report more hunger if they are not rewarded for their fasting than if they are given
        a reward.
    b. they will report little hunger regardless of whether they are given a reward for fasting.
    c. they will report more hunger if they are given $5.00 for their fasting than if they are not
        rewarded.
    d. they will tend to report being very hungry regardless of whether they are given a reward
        for fasting.

15. Which of the following does *not* motivate attitude change (pp. 473-475)?
    a. not performing a behavior because of a mild threat
    b. performing a boring task
    c. performing an interesting activity
    d. suffering to obtain a goal

16. In the Aronson and Carlsmith study, children who received a severe threat concerning what
    would happen if they touched an attractive robot toy rated the toy as attractive while children
    who received a mild threat downgraded the attractiveness of the toy because (p. 475):
    a. children in the severe threat condition could justify avoiding the toy in terms of external
        conditions.
    b. children in the mild threat condition were faced with dissonant cognitions (that the toy was
        attractive and that they did not play with the toy).
    c. children in the mild threat condition could *not* justify avoiding the toy, so they changed
        their cognitions.
    d. all of the above.

17. The process of inferring characteristics from observable behavior is called (p. 476):
    a. the attribution process.
    b. the evaluation process.
    c. the social perception process.
    d. the attitudinal change process.

18. Which of the following is *not* a basis for deciding whether a person's behavior stems from
    internal or external causes (pp. 476-477)?
    a. the distinctiveness of the behavior
    b. knowledge about how other people would respond in the same situation
    c. the frequency of the behavior for that person
    d. the consistency of the behavior for that person

19. According to Jones and Davis, we determine the intentions of individuals by judging their
    (p. 478):
    a. knowledge.
    b. ability.
    c. both a and b above.
    d. none of the above.

20. The degree to which a person's behavior is rewarding or costly to the observer is called
    (p. 478):
    a. hedonic relevance.
    b. the reward/cost radio.
    c. fundamental attribution.
    d. intentional relevance.

21. Your friend is extremely ill. You are driving her to the hospital. You hit a parked car on the
    way but do not stop. An observer labels you a "hit and run" driver and thinks very poorly of
    you. The observer is making (p. 479):
    a. a "hedonic relevance" error.
    b. a fundamental attribution error.
    c. an "intentional knowledge" error.
    d. all of the above.

22. The actor/observer difference in evaluating behavior can be attributed to (p. 480):
    a. the fact that people have more information about themselves than about others.
    b. the fact that personal cues are more salient when we consider our own behavior.
    c. the fact that situational cues are more salient when we consider our own behavior.
    d. both a and c above.

23. The fact that people tend to base their impressions of others on what they first hear about
    them is called (p. 480):
    a. the order effect.
    b. the primacy effect.
    c. the recency effect.
    d. the attribution effect.

24. Two individuals are taking a test. Individual A starts off well but misses several questions at the
    end. Individual B starts off poorly but gets better at the end. Both individuals score the same on
    the test. Who would be evaluated as more intelligent?
    a. They would be evaluated as equally intelligent.
    b. individual A
    c. individual B
    d. They would be evaluated negatively.

25. Rosenthal and Johnson randomly selected some students and labeled them "high achievers."
    At the end of the school year, the students' IQs were measured. The results showed that
    (p. 482):
    a. the label "high achiever" influenced the teachers' expectancies of the students' performance.
    b. the "high achievers" outperformed the other students in terms of IQ scores.
    c. the "high achievers" were part of a "self-fulfilling prophecy."
    d. all of the above.

26. When "self-fulfilling prophecy" occurs (p. 482):
    a. both the actors and observers are aware it is occurring.
    b. only the actors are aware it is occurring.
    c. only the observers are aware it is occurring.
    d. it occurs without the awareness of either party involved.

27. Suppose you overhear a new acquaintance making remarks about you. You would be most
    likely to evaluate that acquaintance positively (say you like him) if (p. 483):
    a. all his comments are positive.
    b. he begins with positive comments and then switches to negative ones.
    c. he begins with negative comments and then switches to positive ones.
    d. all of his comments are neutral.

28. The fact that a need for positive reward is created when someone makes negative statements about you helps explain (p. 484):
   a. the foot-in-the-door effect.
   b. the gain-loss effect.
   c. the primacy effect.
   d. the door-in-the-face effect.

29. People are *not* attracted to one another typically if (pp. 484-485):
   a. they possess similar personality traits.
   b. they possess different personality traits.
   c. they are similar in a way that one does not admire.
   d. they are similar in background.

30. In the Festinger, Schachter, and Back study of friendships is a married-student housing project (p. 486):
   a. residents were most friendly with their next-door neighbors.
   b. residents were most friendly with their neighbors down the hall.
   c. residents were friendly with people in close proximity because they purposely moved in next to their friends.
   d. both a and c above.

31. Studies of physical attractiveness suggest that (pp. 486-488):
   a. we tend to like attractive people more than unattractive ones.
   b. people of average or less-than-average attractiveness are almost always doomed to a life of loneliness.
   c. we tend to become romanticaly involved with people who are less attractive than we are.
   d. we tend to become romantically involved with people who are more attractive than we are.

32. We tend to like people who (pp. 483-488):
   a. reward us.
   b. are around us when good things happen.
   c. live close to us.
   d. all of the above.

33. Which of the following is *not* a step in the decision to help someone (p. 489)?
   a. noticing the person in distress
   b. being an ethical person
   c. interpreting the situation as an emergency
   d. deciding that you have a responsibility to help

34. Someone has just collapsed on a bus. He is most likely to be helped by (p. 489):
   a. someone sitting at the other end of the bus.
   b. someone who was sitting close but then moved further away.
   c. someone seated near the victim.
   d. none of the above.

35. A woman is being attacked by a male assailant. Male bystanders are not coming to her rescue.
    What should she yell at her assailant (p. 489)?
    a. "Please stop it."
    b. "You horrible man."
    c. "What a terrible husband you are."
    d. "I don't know you."

36. Darley and Latane had subjects communicate from private booths. When the subjects believed
    one of the communicators had just suffered a seizure, they were most likely to come to his aid
    when (p. 491):
    a. they thought there were two people in the group.
    b. they thought there were three people in the group.
    c. they thought there were six people in the group.
    d. they thought there were ten people in the group.

37. In very large groups, people may not help a victim because of (p. 491):
    a. lack of notice of the victim's plight.
    b. diffusion of responsibility.
    c. not wanting to help.
    d. none of the above.

38. Bystanders would be most likely to help (p. 492):
    a. a drunk victim.
    b. a victim on drugs.
    c. a victim being threatened by someone very dangerous.
    d. an ill victim.

39. People may react negatively when we try to help them because (pp. 493-494):
    a. they do not like to feel obligated to the helper.
    b. they do not want to admit incompetence.
    c. both a and b above.
    d. neither a nor b above.

40. You are most likely to like (p. 493):
    a. someone who can help you.
    b. someone who can cooperate with you on an equal basis.
    c. both a and b above.
    d. neither a nor b above.

1. b	11. a	21. b	31. a
2. a	12. b	22. d	32. d
3. d	13. a	23. b	33. b
4. c	14. c	24. a	34. c
5. d	15. c	25. d	35. d
6. d	16. d	26. d	36. a
7. b	17. a	27. b	37. b
8. d	18. c	28. b	38. d
9. c	19. c	29. c	39. c
10. b	20. a	30. a	40. b

THOUGHT QUESTIONS/APPLICATIONS

1. In the beginning of the chapter, you learned about how attitudes develop and can be changed. At the end of the chapter, you learned that bystanders often fail to intervene when people are in danger or distress. How might an advertiser interested in the public's welfare use our knowledge of social psychology to get people to adopt a helpful attitude toward people in distress?

2. Try to think of a friend or acquaintance that made a negative first impression but later impressed you favorably. How difficult was it to "undo" that first impression? Why do you think first impressions are so difficult to change?

3. Make a list of the traits you find attractive in other people. How many of them are traits you have yourself? Are your friends birds of a feather? What traits do you find particularly annoying in others? Are they traits you possess?

4. A friend of yours is applying for a job that requires a high degree of intelligence. What advice would you give your friend to help him or her appear intelligent during the interview? Have you ever misjudged someone's intelligence on the basis of surface characteristics and then had to re-evaluate the person when you got to know him or her?

15

The Individual in Groups

CHAPTER OUTLINE

CHAPTER OBJECTIVES

After completing Chapter 15, you should:

1. Be able to explain how belonging to a close-knit group changed Josh Gibson.

2. Be able to describe three reasons why people belong to groups.

3. Know the difference between norms and roles and how both influence our behavior.

4. Understand how informational pressure and normative social pressure lead people to conform.

5. Know the factors that influence a person's tendency to conform to group norms, including group size and whether or not the group is unanimous in its opinion.

6. Be able to discuss the shocking results of the Milgram study of obedience to authority and why people have questioned whether the study was ethical.

7. Be able to distinguish between a "task-specialist" leader and a "socioemotional" leader. What are the different roles that these two leaders play in a group?

8. Understand that the "contingency model" of leadership represents a compromise between the "trait" theory and "situational" theory.

9. Know the difference between a "task-oriented" leader and a "relationship-motivated" leader. Under what circumstances is each style of leadership most effective ?

10. Realize that deindividuation can have positive as well as negative effects on the members of a group.

11. Understand why deindividuation had such a powerful negative effect in Zimbardo's prison study.

12. Understand why group polarization tends to occur and how diffusion of responsibility, social comparison, and persuasive arguments might play a role in polarization.

13. Know what *groupthink* is and how it can be reduced.

14. Be able to contrast socal facilitation and social loafing. Are these two processes totally contradictory?

15. Know the difference between prejudice ad discrimination.

16. See how prejudice and discrimination are heightened by group formation.

17. Be able to contrast learning and scapegoat theories of prejudice and discrimination.

18. Know that reducing prejudice is not quite as simple as having two groups interact in non-competitive situations.

KEY TERMS SELF-TEST

In each group below, fill in the letter of the term on the right with the appropriate definition on the left.

Belonging to Groups I

Definitions

      C 1. two or more persons interacting so that each influences the other

      D 2. beliefs, attitudes, and behaviors of other people

      E 3. using social reality to evaluate oneself by comparing oneself with other people

      A 4. rules that govern specific behavior and apply to all members of a group

      G 5. group rules that apply only to certain members of a group and that define the obligations and expectations of a specific position

      B 6. when a person changes behavior or attitudes as a result of group pressures

      F 7. influence of a group based on its value as a source of information

Key Terms

a. norms (p. 503)
b. conformity (p. 506)
c. group (p. 500)
d. social reality (p. 501)
e. social comparison (p. 501)
f. informational pressure (p. 507)
g. roles (p. 503)

Belonging to Groups II

Definitions

      ~~A~~ **E** 1. type of group pressure based on the desire to belong to the group

      ~~A~~ **D** 2. the following of direct orders of a person in a position of authority

      ~~B~~ **C** 3. when people in groups lose their personal identity and assume the identity of the group

Key Terms

a. groupthink (p. 526)
b. group polarization (p. 524)
c. deindividuation (p. 520)
d. obedience (p. 512)
e. normative social pressure (p. 508)

4. tendency of groups to move people to believe more strongly in the positions that they first held

5. when group members become so concerned with agreeing that they fail to evaluate their idea critically

Performing in Groups, Prejudice, and Discrimination

Definitions

1. the presence of other people arouses people, thus facilitating the performance of well-learned behaviors

2. decrease of motivation of people in groups in which individual performance cannot be observed

3. an unjusted negative attitude toward an individual based soley on that person's membership in a group

4. negative, often aggressive, behavior aimed at the target of prejudice

Key Terms

a. social facilitation (p. 528)
b. prejudice (p. 530)
c. social loafing (p. 529)
d. discrimination (p. 530)

Answers to Key Terms Self-Test

Belonging to Groups I
1. c   5. g
2. d   6. b
3. e   7. f
4. a

Belonging to Groups II
1. e   4. b
2. d   5. a
3. c

Performing in Groups, Prejudice, and Discrimination
1. a
2. c
3. b
4. d

Circle the correct letter.

1. The rewards of belonging to a group include (p. 500):
   a. security.
   b. prestige.
   c. recognition.
   d. all of the above.

2. One of the main reasons people join groups is for (p. 501):
   a. social comparison.
   b. social reality.
   c. deindividuation.
   d. none of the above.

3. Mary is a beginning bridge player. She would be most likely to join a group of (p. 502):
   a. experts.
   b. moderately good players.
   c. other beginners.
   d. mixed-level bridge players.

4. _______________________ specify *what* must be done *when* (p. 503).
   a. Roles
   b. Goals
   c. Norms
   d. Groups

5. In the Roethlisberger and Dickson study of workers on a production line workers were subjected to "binging," a forceful hit on the shoulder, when they (p. 503):
   a. were producing too much.
   b. were producing too little.
   c. deviated from group norms.
   d. all of the above.

6. Roles differ from norms in that roles additionally specify (pp. 503-504):
   a. what must be done.
   b. how it should be done.
   c. who must do it.
   d. when it must be done.

7. Stereotypes about women are becoming (p. 505):
   a. a thing of the past.
   b. less negative.
   c. more negative.
   d. much more frequent.

8. Which of the following is *not* an example of conformity (p. 506)?
   a. Mary adopts the current "jargon" of her sorority sisters, including words she does not feel comfortable saying.
   b. Jack starts wearing button-down shrits to class even though he feels a little silly in them because "everyone is wearing them."
   c. Joan's friends tease her about being too chicken to try marijuana so she finally tries it.
   d. Sarah decides her hair is too long and gets it cut; her friends compliment her on the new style.

9. Conformity (pp. 506-507):
   a. can create problems when there is too little of it.
   b. is always a dangerous thing.
   c. almost always plays a positive role in society.
   d. none of the above.

10. A young boy's family tells him not to touch a hot stove. He disregards the advice and is burnt. In the future, he is more willing to listen to his family's advice. The family now (p. 507):
   a. is exerting normative social pressure.
   b. is exerting informational pressure.
   c. is exerting attitudinal pressure.
   d. is exerting adherence pressure.

11. In Asch's study, six confederate subjects incorrectly choose the line that matches a presented line. The target subject then (p. 509):
   a. always chooses the correct line.
   b. chooses the incorrect (conforming) line 35 percent of the time.
   c. always chooses the incorrect line.
   d. chooses the incorrect (conforming) line 85 percent of the time.

12. Research has shown that men are (pp. 509-510):
   a. more conforming than women.
   b. less conforming than women.
   c. more conforming than women on female-related tasks only.
   d. more conforming than women on male-related tasks only.

13. Research suggests that conformity will be greatest among people who (p. 510):
   a. expect future interaction with group members.
   b. are only mildly attracted to the group.
   c. feel completely accepted by the group.
   d. have been members of the group for a very long period of time.

14. The number of people in a group that produces maximum conformity (p. 511):
    a. is always four.
    b. is always between six and eight.
    c. can be any number since number does not influence conformity.
    d. depends on the setting and other task and group variables.

15. Results of Milgram's experiment indicated that (pp. 512-513):
    a. no normal subjects will blindly obey an authority figure.
    b. no highly educated subjects will blindly obey an authority figure.
    c. only subjects under the age of 40 will blindly obey an authority figure.
    d. all normal subjects, regardless of age or education, will blindly obey an authority figure.

16. When Milgram repeated his experiment in a rundown office building and the experimenter did not wear a lab coat or say he was affiliated with Yale University, (p. 513):
    a. blind obedience to authority dropped off dramatically compared to the original Milgram experiment.
    b. blind obedience was almost as high as in the original experiment.
    c. subjects refused even to participate in the experiment.
    d. none of the above.

17. In a study involving hospital nurses (p. 514):
    a. nurses obeyed orders only when they were in line with hospital rules.
    b. nurses obeyed orders only when they were in line with the maximum safe dosage of the drug being administered.
    c. nurses obeyed the doctor's orders even when they violated both hospital rules and the maximum safe dosage of the drug being administered.
    d. none of the above.

18. In a follow-up questionnaire sent to subjects who had participated in Milgram's study (p. 515):
    a. subjects uniformly reported that they wished they had *not* participated in the experiment.
    b. subjects reported that participation in the experiment had been pleasant.
    c. subjects reported that they were glad they had participated in the experiment despite the fact that the same subjects had appeared very stressed during the experiment.
    d. subjects reported that their participation in the experiment had been unethical.

19. The leader of a group is the person (pp. 515-516):
    a. who has been with the group the longest.
    b. who runs group meetings.
    c. who has the greatest influence on the activities of the group.
    d. all of the above.

20. There are often two leaders in a group. One of the leaders, called the ________________,
    has a strong influence on the person-oriented activities of the group (p. 516).
    a. task specialist
    b. individualist leader
    c. *de facto* leader
    d. socioemotional leaders

21. The phrase that "leaders are born not made" might be endorsed by (p. 516):
    a. great man theorists.
    b. trait theorists.
    c. situational theorists.
    d. both a and b above.

22. Leaders tend to differ from other group members in terms of their (pp. 516-517):
    a. height.
    b. talkativeness.
    c. both a and b.
    d. neither a nor b.

23. The fact that President Johnson was probably more effective in getting the Kennedy reforms
    through Congress than Kennedy himself would have been supports (pp. 517-518):
    a. great man theories of leadership.
    b. situational theories of leadership.
    c. trait theories of leadership.
    d. almost any theory of leadership.

24. Task-oriented leaders are most effective when group climate is (p. 520):
    a. very favorable.
    b. very unfavorable.
    c. moderate.
    d. both a and b above.

25. Deindividuation is most likely to occur when (p. 521):
    a. groups are large.
    b. members of the group can be personally identified.
    c. people are in familiar settings.
    d. people are at very low levels of arousal.

26. One can conclude from Zimbardo's study that (pp. 521-522):
    a. prison guards are tyrannical.
    b. deindividuation can result in destructive behavior.
    c. prison inmates are dehumanized robots.
    d. none of the above.

27. The results of studies of mock juries indicate that (p. 523):
    a. six-person and twelve-person juries generally arrive at the same verdict.
    b. juries required to make unanimous decisions are more likely to judge a person innocent
       than juries required to make two-thirds majority decisions.
    c. it takes juries required to make two-thirds majority decisions just as long to deliberate as
       juries required to make unanimous decisions.
    d. most of the discussion in juries is devoted to testimony presented during the trial.

28. Studies concerning group decision-making have shown that (p. 524):
    a. group decisions are more extreme than individual decisions.
    b. group polarization effects occur.
    c. although groups influence decision-making processes, individuals revert to their original
       decisions when they leave the group.
    d. both a and b above.

29. The fact that group polarization increases when you increase information about why people
    adopted a certain position supports the (p. 525):
    a. diffusion-of-responsibility explanation for polarization.
    b. persuasive-argument explanation for polarization.
    c. social-comparison explanation for polarization.
    d. groupthink explanation for polarization.

30. Groupthink occurs because (p. 526):
    a. membess fail to evaluate critically their ideas.
    b. members try to use too much of the available information.
    c. members feel alienated from one another.
    d. the leader of the group is not strong or forceful enough.

31. Which of the following is *not* good advice for avoiding the groupthink effect (p. 527)?
    a. Encourage members to play the role of devil's advocate.
    b. Invite outsiders to give their opinions.
    c. Have the leader state a strong preference from the outset.
    d. Call a meeting to reassess previous decisions.

32. The fact that people work faster together than when alone is called (pp. 527-528):
    a. social inhibition.
    b. social facilitation.
    c. social loafing.
    d. social complexity.

33. The arousal produced by being in a group inhibits or interferes with (p. 528):
    a. performing well-learned responses.
    b. learning new and complex behaviors.
    c. both a and b above.
    d. neither a nor b above.

34. A person is put in a small group and asked to cheer as loudly as she can. She is then put in a larger group. Which of the following is likely to happen (p. 529)?
   a. The woman will cheer more loudly in the larger group.
   b. The woman will cheer more loudly in the smaller group.
   c. The woman will tend to engage in "social loafing" in the larger group.
   d. both b and c above.

35. Mary has been excluded from a social club because she is Jewish. She has been subjected to (p. 530):
   a. prejudice.
   b. discrimination.
   c. group formation.
   d. none of the above.

36. Which of the following is *not* true about prejudice and discrimination (pp. 530-531)?
   a. Prejudice is usually the function of extensive interaction with the target of the prejudice.
   b. Discrimination is often practiced even when it hurts the person practicing it.
   c. The target of prejudice often takes on the prejudicial attitudes.
   d. Prejudice is baseless.

37. Members of a group (pp. 532-533):
   a. see ingroup members as being different from one another.
   b. see outgroup members as being relatively similar.
   c. feel they can judge all outgroup members by observing just a few.
   d. all of the above.

38. According to the scapegoat theory, prejudice and discrimination are a result of (p. 534):
   a. frustration.
   b. religion.
   c. imitation.
   d. reinforcement.

39. Minority groups are targeted for aggression and hostility because (p. 534):
   a. they are a "safe" target for attack.
   b. they are so powerful.
   c. they have highly visible characteristics that often separate them from the majority.
   d. both a and c above.

40. The Sherif study of children at summer camp showed that (p. 535):
   a. simple contact can reduce intergroup hostility.
   b. assigning children to competitive groups does *not* lead to hostility.
   c. to reduce intergroup hostility groups might work together to solve a common problem.
   d. none of the above.

1. d	11. b	21. d	31. c
2. a	12. c	22. c	32. b
3. c	13. a	23. b	33. b
4. c	14. d	24. d	34. d
5. d	15. d	25. a	35. b
6. b	16. b	26. b	36. a
7. d	17. c	27. a	37. d
8. a	18. c	28. d	38. d
9. a	19. c	29. b	39. d
10. b	20. d	30. a	40. c

THOUGHT QUESTIONS/APPLICATIONS

1. How many groups do you think you belong to? Using your textbook's definition of what a group is, list all the groups to which you belong (remember to include family in the list). Rank order your groups according to how much they influence your beliefs, attitudes, and behavior. Why do some of the groups have a greater influence than others? In answering this question, consider factors such as size of the group, similarity between yourself and other group members, desirability of belonging to the group, and so forth.

2. Conformity and obedience to authority can often be destructive things as shown in the Zimbardo prison study and Milgram's experiment. Try to imagine what the world would be like *without* conformity and obedience to authority. How do these processes *aid* the functioning of society?

3. Suppose an important decision in your life (who you should marry, where you should work, etc.) is to be made by a group of people. How would you structure the group to make the best decision possible and avoid problems such as group polarization, groupthink, deindividuation, and so forth?

4. All of us have prejudicial attitudes. Try to identify one of your strongest prejudices. Does this prejudice actually lead to discrimination on your part against the target of your prejudice? How do think your prejudice developed? Try to list the influences that led you to this prejudicial attitude. Be as *objective* as possible, trying to view your attitude as an outsider *without* the prejudice would.

16

Living with Our Environment

CHAPTER OUTLINE

CHAPTER OBJECTIVES

After completing Chapter 16, you should:

1. Understand why Nino Chochise's adjustment to life outside Pa-Gotzin-Kay was so difficult from an "environmental psychology" perspective.

2. Know why it is so difficult to get people to conserve energy and have some ideas about how this difficulty can be overcome.

3. Be able to distinguish among primary territories, secondary territories, and public territories and be able to categorize the "spaces" in your life into these three territories.

4. Know the four interaction distances and the kinds of social activities that occur at each distance.

5. Be aware that cultural background has a big impact on interaction distances and know what that impact is for various cultures.

6. Be able to describe a typical person's response to invasion of his or her personal space. What is your response?

7. Be able to interpret the adage "Good fences make good neighbors" in terms of the functions of territory.

8. Realize that sound and density are physical characteristics while noise and crowding are psychological states.

9. Be able to compare the response of rat and human populations to situations in which crowding occurs.

10. Realize that crowding is more than a function of the number of people in a given space. Factors such as having a friend present, having control over the environment, and so forth can influence one's perception of crowding.

11. Be able to describe the effects crowding and noise have on task performance and other behavior.

12. Be aware that noise may present a particularly acute problem for children exposed to it on a long-term basis.

13. Be able to present arguments against the hypothesis that air pollution only has negative effects if you are exposed to it for long periods of time.

14. Know that weather can play a very subtle role in our lives, influencing our behavior and task performance.

15. Understand that a room's shape, color and attractiveness, and furniture arrangement can influence our perception of that room and our behavior in it.

16. Be able to describe the shortcomings of living in a high-rise and how architects can overcome some of those shortcomings through careful designing.

17. Understand why cities lead to "cognitive overload" and how people in cities respond to over-stimulation. What consequences do their responses have in terms of their friendliness to strangers?

In each group below, fill in the letter of the term on the right with the appropriate definition on the left

Environmental Psychology and Territoriality

Definitions

1. subfield of psychology that emphasizes how behavior is influenced by environmental factors

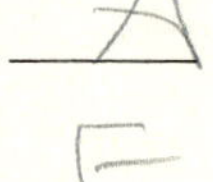

2. the claiming of control or ownership of areas or objects

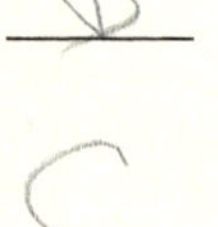

3. owned and controlled by people, these territories are central to their lives

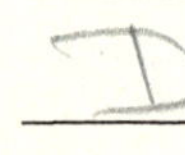

4. not owned by people, these territories are not as central to their lives

5. territories that do not involve a feeling of ownership but that people feel they control

Key Terms

a. territoriality (p. 545)
b. secondary territory (p. 546)
c. public territory (p. 547)
d. environmental psychology (p. 543)
e. primary territory (p. 546)

Personal, Space, Density, and Crowding

Definitions

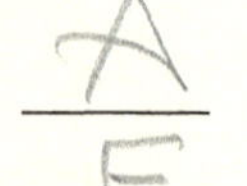

1. an area directly surrounding one's body that is regarded as personal territory

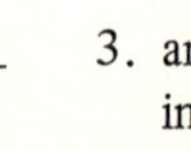

2. study of personal space

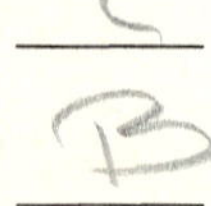

3. amount of space between people in various situations

4. a measure of the number of people in a given area

5. psychological state that often, but not always, accompanies high density

Key Terms

a. proxemics (p. 550)
b. crowding (p. 554)
c. density (p. 554)
d. personal space (p. 550)
e. interaction distance (p. 550)

Definitions   **Key Terms**

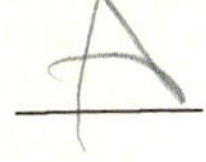 1. a physical property caused by
changes in air pressure, measured
in decibels

 2. a psychological concept, sound that
is unpleasant

 3. area in apartment complex not open
to observation

 4. an inability to respond to stimuli
because there are too many events
occurring in the environment

a. sound (p. 560)
b. cognitive overload (p. 571)
c. noise (p. 560)
d. indefensible space (p. 568)

Answers to Key Terms Self-Test

Environmental Psychology and Territoriality
1. d   4. b
2. a   5. c
3. e

Personal Space, Density, and Crowding
1. d   4. c
2. a   5. b
3. e

Other Environmental Variables and the Built Environment
1. a
2. c
3. d
4. b

PRACTICE TEST

Circle the correct letter.

1. The subfield of psychology that aims to examine the relationship between the physical
   environment and human behavior is called (p. 543):
   a. environmental psychology.
   b. physical psychology.
   c. engineering psychology.
   d. social psychology.

2. In some cases, the physical intensity of the environment is not as important as the degree of

____________________________ a person has (p. 545):
   a. predictability
   b. control
   c. both a and b above
   d. none of the above

3. The energy question can be seen as a "social trap" because (p. 544):
   a. people do not receive feedback about their energy consumption.
   b. people believe the problem is so large that they cannot help by conserving.
   c. energy behaviors that help the individual hurt the group.
   d. all of the above.

4. Fences, hedges, and walkways are all signs of (p. 546):
   a. instinct.
   b. defensive precautions.
   c. aggression.
   d. human territoriality.

5. Which of the following is *not* a difference between the way in which animals and humans treat territory (p. 546)?
   a. Animal territorial behavior tends to be innate, whereas human territorial behavior tends to be learned.
   b. Animals are much more "territorial" than humans.
   c. Animals claim territory only while they occupy it, whereas humans claim territory they do not occupy.
   d. Humans consider more things and places as part of their territory than animals.

6. Mary always sits in the seat closest to the door in class. This seat is an example of (pp. 546-547):
   a. primary territory.
   b. secondary territory.
   c. public territory.
   d. private territory.

7. The fact that Americans and Europeans behave differently in restaurants and have different ideas about who "controls" tables in restaurants reflects basic differences in (p. 547):
   a. primary territory.
   b. secondary territory.
   c. public territory.
   d. private territory.

8. Spacing, protection, and identity are all advantages or functions of (pp. 548-549):
   a. territory.
   b. personal space.
   c. interaction distance.
   d. interpersonal distance.

9. In a study of human territory, pairs of subjects were asked to work on tasks in the room of one of the subjects. The research indicated that (p. 549):
   a. the resident subject tended to dominate the interaction.
   b. the visitor subject assumed the role of leader.
   c. the resident subject assumed the role of leader.
   d. both a and c above.

10. The "home-court" advantage of territory (pp. 548-549):
   a. is largely a myth.
   b. may explain some military victories in which the better equipped army lost to the resident army.
   c. can be seen only in athletic contests.
   d. is easily overcome.

11. Which of the following orderings of interaction distances (from close to far) is correct (p. 550)?
   a. intimate, personal, social
   b. personal, intimate, social
   c. intimate, public, social
   d. social, personal, public

12. According to Hall's work with interaction distances, most people discuss business using the

   _____________________ distance (p. 550):
   a. public
   b. intimate
   c. social
   d. personal

13. Research has shown that the shape of an interpersonal space zone is (p. 550):
   a. circular.
   b. square.
   c. rectangular.
   d. egg-shaped.

14. By communicating at an "intimate" distance (p. 551):
   a. facial details, muscle twitches, and eye contact can facilitate communication.
   b. certain channels of communication, such as body posture, are closed.
   c. you are probably showing the other person that you like him or her.
   d. all of the above.

15. You are at an internationally attended party. Who is most likely to stand the closest to you while talking (p. 551)?
    a. an American
    b. a Latin American
    c. a German
    d. an Englishman

16. Females (p. 552):
    a. have closer personal spaces than males in all situations.
    b. have closer personal spaces when interacting with familiar males (mixed-sex pair) than with familiar females (same-sex pair).
    c. have closer personal spaces with a strange male than with a strange female.
    d. seem oblivious to the fact that intimacy can be communicated by spacing.

17. Byrne showed that men seated at a library table were most disturbed by (pp. 552-553):
    a. a stranger taking the seat opposite them.
    b. a stranger taking the seat to the left of them.
    c. a stranger taking the seat to the right of them.
    d. a beautiful female seating herself anywhere near them.

18. A stranger is invading your personal space at a party. Finally, the stranger backs you into a corner. You are likely to (p. 553):
    a. stare at the stranger.
    b. face the stranger directly.
    c. lean toward the stranger.
    d. fold your arms in front of you.

19. If you divided the population of your town by its area, you would be getting a measure of (p. 554):
    a. behavioral sinks.
    b. crowding.
    c. personal space.
    d. density.

20. John Calhoun's study of crowding in rat pens showed that (pp. 554-555):
    a. the rats distributed themselves evenly among four pens.
    b. only abnormal *psychological* effects occurred; the health of the rats was not affected.
    c. females suffered from a large number of miscarriages and other health problems.
    d. the maternal behavior of females was not affected.

21. Amy is doing her last-minute Christmas shopping and the stores are overcrowded. Amy would probably PERCEIVE the situation as less crowded if (p. 556):
    a. she were a male.
    b. she had a large personal space zone.
    c. she were shopping with a friend and could focus her attention on the friend.
    d. she could use her home-court advantage.

22. Wicker has a somewhat novel approach to the question of crowding. He feels crowding is a function of (p. 557):
    a. the number of people in the environment.
    b. the space in the environment.
    c. density.
    d. none of the above.

23. In the Freedman study, students were put in crowded or noncrowded rooms and asked to listen to tapes of court cases involving violent crimes. The results of the study indicated that (p. 558):
    a. females were always assigned milder sentences than males.
    b. males were assigned harsher sentences when they were in crowded rooms.
    c. females were assigned harsher sentences when they were in crowded rooms.
    d. crowding had no effect on the harshness of sentences assigned.

24. Given the same density of people in a room, people will feel *less* crowded if (p. 559):
    a. they believe they can leave the room if they want to.
    b. there are *not* any pictures on the wall.
    c. there *are* pictures on the wall.
    d. both a and c above.

25. Research has been conducted on the differences between suite-type dormitories and corridor-type dormitories. The results suggest that (p. 569):
    a. students in corridor rooms feel more crowded.
    b. students in suite rooms feel a greater sense of privacy.
    c. suite residents feel more control over their lives.
    d. all of the above.

26. The physical property caused by changes in air pressure is called (p. 560):
    a. sound.
    b. noise.
    c. both a and b above.
    d. none of the above.

27. Seventy-year old Sudanese tribesmen have hearing sensitivity comparable to (p. 561):
    a. 70-year olds living in the United States.
    b. 85-year olds living in the United States.
    c. 50-year olds living in the United States.
    d. 20-year olds living in the United States.

28. The study of Cohen, Glass, and Singer concerning reading abilities of children living in various
    environments showed (p. 562):
    a. children living on lower floors of a high-rise were exposed to more highway noise than
        children living on upper floors.
    b. children living on lower floors had lower reading abilities than those living on upper floors.
    c. there were no differences between children living on lower and higher floors in their reading
        abilities.
    d. both a and b above.

29. A study in England involving air from automobile exhaust pipes demonstrated that (pp. 563-
    564):
    a. pollution had no effect on subjects' task performance.
    b. air pollution only has an effect when subjects are exposed for long periods of time, perhaps
        years.
    c. air pollution can have short-term effects on behavior such as task performance.
    d. none of the above.

30. Excessive heat can be associated with (p. 565):
    a. poor performance on tasks involving concentration and psychomotor skills.
    b. increasingly hostile tempers.
    c. a decline in social interaction when it is combined with other frustrations.
    d. all of the above.

31. Lieber and Sherin conducted a study concerning the influence of phases of the moon on human
    behavior. They found (p. 565):
    a. no relationship between behavior and moon phases.
    b. that homicides were more frequent during new- and full-moon phases.
    c. that homicides were less frequent during new- and full-moon phases.
    d. that, paradoxically, the phases of the moon that cause the greatest ocean disturbances have
        the least effect on human behavior.

32. Research has shown that the shape of rooms and the number of doors and windows have an
    effect on how crowded the room is perceived. Which of the following rooms would seem *most*
    crowded given the same number of people in each room (p. 566)?
    a. a square room with one door and no windows
    b. a square room with two doors and one window
    c. a rectangular room with one door and no windows
    d. a rectangular room with two doors and one window

33. If two people are put in a competitive situation, they prefer to be seated (p. 567):
    a. side by side.
    b. corner to corner.
    c. face to face.
    d. back to back.

34. High-rise residents (p. 568):
    a. form fewer relationships with other residents than low-rise residents.
    b. trust their neighbors more than low-rise residents.
    c. are more willing to help their neighbors than low-rise residents.
    d. all of the above.

35. Alleys, enclosed stairways, and other areas that are not open to observation are called (p. 568):
    a. dark spaces.
    b. indefensible spaces.
    c. personal spaces.
    d. secondary territories.

36. The "flight to the suburbs" (pp. 570-571):
    a. is continuing full force.
    b. may be reversing.
    c. may be influenced by the energy crisis.
    d. both b and c above.

37. Cognitive overload can result in (p. 571):
    a. stress or psychological breakdown.
    b. Parkinson's disease.
    c. brain disease.
    d. heart failure.

38. People in cities respond to overstimulation by (p. 571):
    a. giving more time to each event.
    b. dealing with situations more quickly.
    c. paying more attention to details.
    d. giving all inputs equal weight.

39. Milgram had students walk down a street in a big city or small town and extend a friendly
    handshake to strangers. He found that (pp. 571-572):
    a. strangers in big cities were just as likely to accept the handshake as small-town strangers.
    b. strangers in big cities accepted the handshake about one-third of the time.
    c. strangers in small towns accepted the handshake about two-thirds of the time.
    d. both b and c above.

40. Suppose you needed to use a telephone and you asked a stranger if you could use his or hers.
    You would have the best chance at gaining entry into the stranger's home if (p. 572):
    a. you were a female and asking in Manhattan.
    b. you were a female and asking in a small town.
    c. you were a male and asking in a small town.
    d. you were a male and asking in Manhattan.

1. a	11. a	21. c	31. b
2. c	12. c	22. a	32. a
3. c	13. d	23. b	33. c
4. d	14. d	24. d	34. a
5. b	15. b	25. d	35. b
6. b	16. b	26. a	36. d
7. c	17. a	27. d	37. a
8. a	18. d	28. d	38. b
9. d	19. d	29. c	39. d
10. b	20. c	30. d	40. b

THOUGHT QUESTIONS/APPLICATIONS

1. Make a list of all of the living "spaces" that you encounter during the average day. Which of these spaces do you see as your "primary" territory? What kind of invasions into this territory cause conflicts in your everyday life? Which spaces are "secondary" territories? "Public" territories? Do you feel you are a particularly "territorial" individual? What kinds of personality characteristics or life experiences might influence how territorial a person is?

2. Undoubtedly everyone is disturbed at least a little when someone invades his or her personal space. However, there are individual differences in a person's response to this invasion. How do you respond when another person "crowds" you? Does it depend on the age of the other person? The sex? Whether or not the other person is an acquaintance or a stranger? Try to remember someone who constantly invades your personal space. Do you like or dislike that person?

3. Try to picture the house you grew up in. Which room in the house do you find most pleasant? How do factors such as the size of the room, the shape, the number of doors and windows, the color and decoration, and the furniture arrangement influence your perception of that room? Would you expect a lot of individual differences in the configuration of these factors that people find most pleasant? Why or why not?

4. Try to remember the last time you were in a crowd of people and *felt* crowded. Now remember the last time you were in a crowd and enjoyed the experience. What factors determined your perceptions of these two experiences?